CYCLE RIDES
in
SHROPSHIRE

CYCLE RIDES
in
SHROPSHIRE

Dave Hancock

2nd edition © David Hancock, 2012

1st edition © David Hancock, 2006

Published by Sigma Leisure – an imprint of
Sigma Press, Stobart House, Pontyclerc, Penybanc Road, Ammanford, Carmarthenshire SA18 3HP.

British Library Cataloguing in Publication Data
A CIP record for this book is available from the British Library.

ISBN: 978-1-85058-934-1

Typesetting and Design by: Sigma Press, Ammanford.

Cover photograph: © David Hancock

Maps and photographs: Dave Hancock

Printed by: TJ International Ltd, Padstow, Cornwall

Disclaimer: the information in this book is given in good faith and is believed to be correct at the time of publication. No responsibility is accepted by either the author or publisher for errors or omissions, or for any loss or injury howsoever caused. Only you can judge your own fitness, competence and experience. Do not rely solely on the sketch maps to navigate, we strongly recommend the use of appropriate Ordnance Survey (or equivalent) maps.

Foreword

In the foreword to the first edition of Cycle Rides in Shropshire, I wrote that the Shropshire countryside invites exploration. Many people responded to that invitation and decided to explore the county by cycle, using the book as their guide.

This second edition will, I am sure, prove equally popular. Certainly Shropshire offers the inquisitive person plenty to interest them. The landscape is very varied, ranging from impressive hills to beautiful, peaceful valleys. One minute you can be cycling past sheep grazing and then just around the next bend a glistening mere stretches ahead of you. Shropshire also has many architectural gems – fine bridges, magnificient castles and stunning country houses.

As one of the least densely populated counties in England, it's no surprise that the country lanes of Shropshire are mostly quiet – making them ideal for cycling. Quite often you'll see more horses and riders, tractors or walkers than you will motorists. There are, of course, hills – the ascent of which could get you puffing a bit. Don't be afraid to dismount and push your cycle – the slower pace is an even better way to admire the views. Fortunately, every hill has a down side, offering the opportunity for a pleasant bit of freewheeling...

Alison Patrick

Alison Patrick
Tourism Officer, Shropshire Council

Preface

A book of cycle rides of varying length that allows readers to explore the beautiful county of Shropshire. Mainly on quiet roads, trails and towpaths, the routes range from easy rides for families with young children to day-long trips for energetic cyclists. There are chapters on Shropshire and places of particular interest, wildlife and plants in the county as well as how to prepare for the cycling rides. Each ride is described with easily understood directions and explanatory narrative.

This second edition includes two additional rides. Ride 21 takes in the area to the south-west of the county bordering Wales in a challenging 25-mile route. Ride 22 is a meander alongside the River Severn in Shrewsbury before looping around the south of the town on quiet country lanes. The section on Shropshire and information such as the costs of parking have also been updated.

Acknowledgements
My thanks to Kylie Bull who drafted the chapters on Shropshire and the wildlife, flora and fauna of the county and to Alison Patrick for writing the foreword.

My partner, Dorothy, read the proofs and gave me endless encouragement, for which I am most grateful.

Dave Hancock

Locations of rides

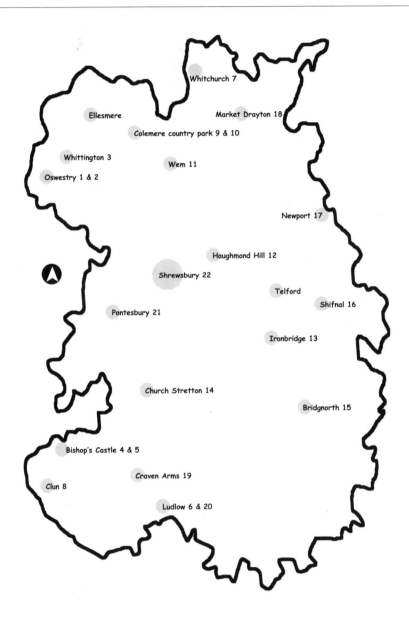

Whitchurch 7

Ellesmere

Market Drayton 18

Colemere country park 9 & 10

Whittington 3

Wem 11

Oswestry 1 & 2

Newport 17

Haughmond Hill 12

Shrewsbury 22

Telford

Shifnal 16

Pontesbury 21

Ironbridge 13

Church Stretton 14

Bridgnorth 15

Bishop's Castle 4 & 5

Craven Arms 19

Clun 8

Ludlow 6 & 20

Contents

Key to rides

No	Title	Distance (miles/km)	Comments
1	Quiet lanes near Oswestry	23.3/37.5	A long family ride with shortcut options
2	North of Oswestry and into Wales	18.5/29.8	Hilly and challenging
3	Whittington north and around the Martins	15.0/24.1	A family ride with one steep hill
4	Bishop's Castle and below The Long Mynd	20.4/32.8	Hilly with spectacular views
5	North of Bishop's Castle through The Bog	29.9/48.1 or 13.8/22.3	A long, hilly route with a shortcut option
6	A loop through the hamlets south of Ludlow	19.9/32.0	Changes of scenery, with a couple of steep ascents and main road crossings
7	South-east of Whitchurch around Shavington Park	23.1/37.2	Mainly level. Passes Brown Moss Nature Reserve. Can be linked to Ride 18
8	From Clun through Clun Forest	17.8/28.6	Many steep hills in a remote part of Shropshire
9	Circuit of the Meres	7.3/11.7	A lovely family ride from Colemere Countryside Heritage Site. Can be linked with Ride 10 or Ride 11
10	Criss-crossing canals around Ellesmere	22.5/36.2	A longer ride for all the family from Colemere Countryside Heritage Site. Can be linked with Ride 9
11	From Wem to Whixall Moss	15.2/24.5	No steep hills and quiet roads - a good family ride. Can be linked with Ride 9

No	Title	Distance (miles/km)	Comments
12	A loop from Haughmond Hill	26.8/43.1	A long but mainly level ride from a lovely picnic site
13	From Ironbridge around The Wrekin	15.6/25.1	Steep ascents from the start with spectacular views
14	From Church Stretton below Wenlock Edge	20.7/33.3	Good views of Wenlock Edge with just a couple of hard hills
15	From Bridgnorth towards the highest point in Shropshire	22.3/35.9	A couple of steep ascents but downhill most of the way back. Take a picnic
16	Shifnal to Blists Hill and back	15.3/24.6	Many miles on traffic-free tracks, so a good family ride. Can be linked with Ride 13
17	Newport to Granville Country Park	23.0/37.0	No steep hills. A longer family ride with just a couple of busy junctions
18	A northern loop from Market Drayton	13.0/20.9	A predominantly level route through pleasant countryside. Can be linked to Ride 7
19	From Craven Arms along a Roman road	15.1/24.3	Hilly, with some steep ascents but excellent views
20	From Ludlow along Corve Dale	24.0/38.6 or 19.0/30.6	A challenging ride with lots of climbing
21	A circular route from Pontesbury	24.6/39.6	Fantastic views with some steep uphill sections
22	Shrewsbury loop	19.6/31.5	Exploring the quiet lanes south of the county town

How to use this book

Cycle rides in Shropshire is for cyclists of all ages and abilities who want to explore the county. The 22 rides are all circular routes which start and finish at easily accessible places across Shropshire. They follow quiet roads, cycle paths and trails wherever possible. There are some off-road sections but none that require a mountain bike. All the routes can be undertaken on a touring bike, a commuter bike or a shopping bike. Those rides that do not include off-road sections could also be tackled on a tricycle, tandem, tandem tricycle or recumbent cycle.

Durable treaded tyres would be a wise choice and for some of the hillier routes in particular you will need a range of ratios – including some low gears (a small chainwheel at the front and large sprockets at the back).

Each ride has straightforward route-finding instructions in the form of a table. Distances are given in miles and shown to two decimal places. This is because the routes were ridden with a GPS-linked odometer. Don't worry if the computer on your cycle is not as accurate – use the distances given to help you identify appropriate junctions. Indeed, you do not even need a cycle computer as the comments for each junction include information such as place names on signposts, the names of roads and obvious landmarks. While it is not necessary to carry the relevant map(s) for each ride, doing so will assist you to find places of interest and vary the route. For each ride, I have included a sketch map. They are not to scale but do give an indication of where the ride goes.

Instructions are only given for junctions where you need to turn – otherwise you should just follow the road. Hopefully, the instructions are self-explanatory. In case they are not, the diagram on the next page tells you what they mean.

Some information about Shropshire follows. However, if you are using these cycle rides to explore the county, you would be well advised to collect information on the aspects that interest you most from a Visitor Information Centre. The contact details for these, as well as other useful contact information, is in Appendix 1 at the back of the book.

Right turn

Left turn

Right @ T

Left @ x-rds

Right/left @ x-rds

Fork left

First exit @ mini-rbt

Right where road goes left

The county of Shropshire

Shropshire is one the least populated counties in England with the estimated population for June 2010 put at 293,400*. The county has a total land mass of 3,487 km², making it the United Kingdom's largest inland county. Shropshire shares its borders with Cheshire, Staffordshire, Worcestershire, Herefordshire, and the Welsh ceremonial counties of Powys and Clwyd. The county is a cyclists' paradise with hundreds of villages, 21 towns – the five largest being Shrewsbury, Telford, Oswestry, Bridgnorth and Ludlow – but no cities.

For visitors and local inhabitants alike, Shropshire offers a wealth of attractions including numerous castles such as the romantic 13th century Stokesay Castle and Ludlow Castle – a fine combination of Norman, Medieval and Tudor architecture. Other attractions include the stately home and gardens at Weston Park, the country's premier steam train railway that wends its way through 16 miles of glorious countryside and restored stations, and Hawkstone Historic Park and Follies – a historic parkland that covers 100 acres and offers some of the finest views of the Shropshire countryside. Hawkstone's magical land of grottoes, caves, cliffs and follies was used as a setting for the Chronicles of Narnia television series.

The county is home to some superb museums, such as the Royal Air Force Museum at Cosford and the living, breathing Blists Hill Victorian Town at Ironbridge – Ironbridge Gorge is a UNESCO World Heritage Site.

Offa's Dyke can be found near Oswestry and the lesser known Mitchell's Fold Stone Circle on the long ridge of Stapeley Hill, 1,000 feet above sea level, is also worth a visit as the site's exposed position gives fine views of the Stiperstones to the east and the Welsh hills to the west.

Shropshire events cover such a diverse range that there is bound to be something for everyone, from the internationally-renowned Shrewsbury Flower Festival to the Darwin Festival (Charles Darwin was born in Shrewsbury) and the Shrewsbury International Cartoon Festival. The county hosts several open air concerts at spectacular venues including Attingham Park, and the town of Bridgnorth hosts the popular English Haydn Music Festival every May.

The Ludlow Marches Food & Drink Festival, the best known annual festival of its kind in Britain, is held every September. The event features more than 120 small producers and suppliers of quality food and drink from Ludlow and the Marches. Ludlow itself has been described as 'a little bit of France near the Welsh border' and with more Michelin Stars than any other town in the UK, it's not hard to see why. For afternoon tea, take a trip to Clungunford and step back into a bygone age at Rocke Cottage Tearooms, winner of the UK Tea Guild's Top Tea Place 2011.

Shropshire is renowned for real ale and micro-breweries – there are 17 small independent breweries in the county, including the Three

Tuns Brewery at Bishop's Castle, which has been happily brewing since 1642. Shrewsbury biscuits are popular worldwide and can be bought freshly baked from bakers and specialist food shops in the town.

Wildlife, flora and fauna

Shropshire is built on rocks from 11 of the 13 known geological periods - the smallest area in the world to claim so many. As the Ice Age ended, glaciers melted and created Shropshire's own Lake District around Ellesmere, one of the most historic and beautiful regions in England. The River Severn meanders majestically through the county, joining canals and trout streams through a patchwork of fields, limestone grassland, lowland raised bog, ancient woodland and heather clad hills. In particular, the hills of South Shropshire are one of the few remaining rural idylls and a designated area of outstanding natural beauty.

Shropshire is also famous for its moss, formed since the last ice age when a kilometre-thick ice sheet covered North Shropshire. The tremendous forces of ice carved the landscape we see today. In their time, the mosses have swallowed up countless mighty oaks and 3,400 years ago, a pine forest grew across their centre, recording past climate change. Man almost destroyed the mosses by drainage for transport, agriculture, forestry and peat cutting, but they were rescued for nature conservation once raised bogs became such a rarity. Ride 7 takes in the Brown Moss nature reserve near Whitchurch, which is considered one of Shropshire's most fascinating locations.

Such diversity of habitat makes Shropshire a haven for wildlife. The county is home to fallow deer, otters, dormice, water voles, badgers, hares, bats, waterfowl, birds of prey, songbirds, dragonflies, countless species of butterfly and even the UK's largest spider, the fish-catching Raft Spider. Hundred of species flourish here and many of England's protected and endangered species can be found in this unspoiled county.

Redstarts, buzzards, chiffchaffs and skylarks provide an idyllic musical milieu for your cycle ride and if you chance to look skywards, you may see the Lapwing, known locally as the 'farmer's friend' performing its aerial acrobatics.

Shropshire Wildlife Trust cares for 37 nature reserves, all of which are open to visitors. In addition, Natural England's Mosses Trails around the north of the county take in the wildlife and special landscape character of the area.

Shropshire's fauna embraces the bold and the beautiful, from majestic oaks to delicate orchids. Wenlock Edge alone boasts nine different orchid varieties.

England's spring and summer classics – bluebells, lilies, hollyhocks, delphiniums, lavender and campanulas will tempt even the most ardent cyclist to stop and smell the flowers.

In the autumn woodlands, you can find edible fungi including Giant Puff Balls and Chicken of the Woods, but extreme caution must be taken and unless you are 100 per cent sure of what you are eating, stick to a packed or pub lunch.

In the spring, much of the ancient woodland cloaking the lower slopes of the Wrekin is carpeted with bluebells along with wood anemone, wood sorrel, toothwort, golden saxifrage and yellow archangel. Ancient yew trees, centuries old, can also be found on the Wrekin alongside mature plantations of beech and sweet chestnut and areas of acidic woodland with silver birch, bilberries and wavy hairgrass.

Preparing for the rides

Ensure your tyres are inflated to the correct pressures and take a puncture repair kit and a pump with you. On some of the rides, there are steep descents so make sure the brakes on your cycle are working properly.

Take plenty of suitable clothing as the weather can change quickly – particularly in the hilly areas. A helmet is not a legal requirement but offers protection if you fall.

Carry plenty of water to drink and snack foods such as bananas and biscuits.

On narrow, winding lanes watch carefully and listen for oncoming traffic and vehicles approaching from behind. Quite often, the other road users will be fellow cyclists, walkers or horse riders. Warn them of your presence (use a bell or call out), slow down, give them plenty of room and say hello – people in Shropshire are generally friendly.

The off-road sections require particular care – cycle slowly in a low gear and be ready to use the brakes. Don't exhaust yourself trying to ride up the steep hills – it's much more pleasant to walk with your cycle and enjoy the views.

* Office for National Statistics, Neighbourhood Statistics

Ride 1: Quiet lanes near Oswestry

A pleasant 23-mile ride around the quiet lanes to the east of Oswestry offering excellent views and picturesque scenery. The ride includes a section alongside the Shropshire Union Canal Montgomeryshire Branch then climbs gently to give fabulous views of the Welsh hills. The start/finish is in Oswestry or at one of two car parks along the route.

This is a lovely ride for a Saturday or Sunday afternoon, which is suitable for all but the youngest members of a family (although shorter variations are possible). Solo riders will also enjoy the peaceful and relaxing countryside. At any time of year, there are many birds and animals to be seen – from greenfinches and rabbits to the occasional hawk.

Mostly, the route is flat but a short climb after about five miles results in a series of spectacular views of the hills of Shropshire and the Berwyn mountain range across the border in Wales. The route returns (at about 13 miles) to offer more splendid views of these hills and mountains.

Part of the route is off road, alongside the Shropshire Union Canal – for which a mountain bike is not necessary. Some parts are a bit bumpy and just need to be approached with caution.

Canal crossings are interesting places to pause

You should note that cycling on towpaths is only permitted by British Waterways on certain sections of canal. In this area, if you have a permit, you can cycle on the towpath from Queen's Head towards Rednal. Alternatively, cycle on the road which runs alongside the canal. At the time of writing, it is not permitted to cycle on the towpath between Maesbury Marsh and Queen's Head – which would make an interesting alternative route for this ride.

This is not a busy section of the Shropshire Union Canal and there are plants and wildlife in abundance. It's worth having a wild flower book with you to help identify the different species. Think about taking a picnic too – alongside the canal is just one of many places to pause on this ride. Alternatively, there are public houses at Maesbury Marsh, Queen's Head, West Felton and Maesbrook.

While in Oswestry, do visit the Heritage Centre (which has an award-winning tea room), the Old Oswestry Fort and the Transport Museum. Regional Cycle Route 31 passes through Oswestry and can be used to explore further afield.

Map	Ordnance Survey 1:50,000 Landranger 126
Distance	23.3 miles (37.5km)
Waymarked	No
Gradients	One steepish hill
Surface	Asphalt, gravel and grass
Shops and refreshments	Oswestry and on route
Permits	A British Waterways cycling permit, for the section of towpath from Queens Head towards Rednal, can be downloaded from www.waterscape.com or telephone British Waterways on 01923 201120. There is an alternative on-road route

Access points
The ride starts and finishes in the centre of Oswestry – the long stay Central Car Park is handy if you arrive by car, although it is height restricted to two metres. The Horsemarket car park by the castle is not height restricted.

Alternatively, you can start and finish at the small public car parks at Queen's Head or one mile north-west of Queen's Head on the way to Rednal. The ride passes each of these places and you can make a minor route change to avoid Oswestry altogether.

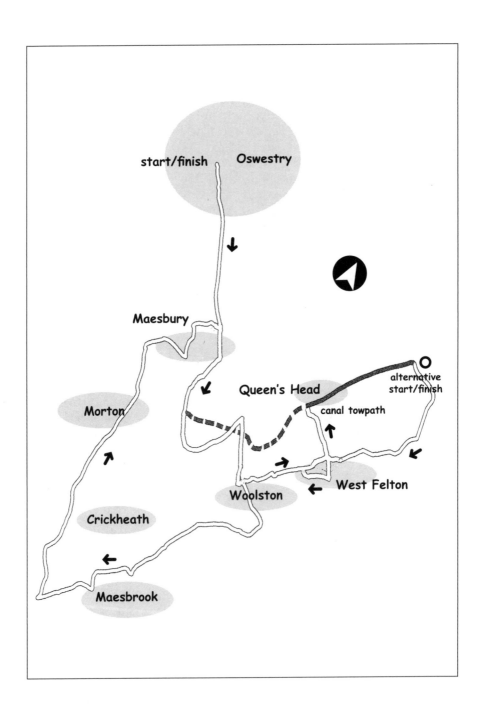

start/finish Oswestry

Maesbury

Queen's Head

alternative
start/finish

canal towpath

Morton

West Felton

Woolston

Crickheath

Maesbrook

The route

Instruction	Miles	Comments
Turn right at road	0.00	From Oswestry Central Car Park, push your cycle out of the entrance and turn right into Salop Road
Fork right	0.51	Signposted Maesbury 3. Shared use cycle/pedestrian pathway option on Maesbury Road through industrial estate. Look out for the Wat's Dyke information board
Right/left @ x-rds	1.36	Use cycle lanes to cross busy A5 road into Maesbury Road. Signposted Maesbury
Right turn	2.44	Into Back Lane. Signposted Newbridge and Morton
Right @ T	2.82	Into Morton Lane
Left	2.93	After bridge over stream, take first left. No signpost. Signed Unsuitable for H.G.Vs
	3.28	Caution on bridge over canal
	3.35	Caution ford - may be fast flowing, use footbridge if necessary
Right @ T	3.86	Caution, main road. No signpost
	4.05	Bridge over canal. It is tempting to turn left onto the towpath and take a pleasant short cut to Queen's Head. However, at the time of writing, cycling is not permitted on this section of towpath. If you wish to walk with your cycle, it is just over two miles to Queen's Head
Left	4.83	After short, steep hill, turn left where road bears right. No signpost
Straight @ x-rds	6.77	Give way. Signposted Grimpo and Rednal. Punch Bowl country inn and village store
Left @ x-rds	6.92	Turn into Twyford Lane. Signposted Twyford and Queens Head
Right @ T	7.63	Give way. Signposted Oswestry and Shrewsbury
Right @ x-rds	7.81	Junction before Queens Head public house. Signposted Hordley and Rednal. Alternative start/finish car park on left

Instruction	Miles	Comments
	7.85	Pass through gates after green corrugated iron barn on left to join towpath (bumpy) or continue along road
Right	8.66	If on towpath, pass under a bridge and go steeply uphill for a few yards. Stop, then take the right turn at the road junction to pass a car park on the left - alternative start/finish. A steady incline is followed by a short steep hill
Fork right	9.24	No signpost
Right @ T	9.71	No signpost
Left @ x-rds	10.43	Junction by school. Turn into Oak Farm Lane. Signposted Eardiston and Wykey
Right @ T	10.72	Signposted West Felton
Straight @ x-rds	11.24	Proceed into Fox Lane.
Straight	11.42	Where road bears left, go straight on (by Applewood Heights sign)
		Cross A5 on narrow bridge
Left @ T	11.66	Turn into Woolston Road. Signposted Woolston and Maesbury
Left	12.27	Turn left where road bends right. Signposted Sandford and Shrewsbury
Right @ x-rds	12.80	Signposted Morton and Llynclys. Pause to admire the views along this road
Straight @ x-rds	13.57	Care crossing road. Signposted The Wood and Maesbrook. Pause for views of the Welsh hills
Straight @ x-rds	13.98	Care crossing main road. Signposted The Wood
Right @ T	15.46	No signpost
Right	16.54	Just after Z bends sign. Signposted Crickheath and Morton
	18.01	Becomes Long Lane

Instruction	Miles	Comments
Straight @ x-rds	18.77	Cross into Morton Lane
Left	19.34	Signposted Upper Sweeney
Right	19.93	Signposted Gwernybrenin (sic)
Left @ x-rds	20.55	Signposted Oswestry
Left @ T	21.30	On to Maesbury Road
Right/left @ x-rds	21.98	Use cycle lanes to cross busy A5 road into industrial estate
		Shared use cycle/pedestrian pathway option through industrial estate
Left @ T	22.83	Continue into centre of Oswestry
Left	23.34	Into Central Car Park

Ride 2 : North of Oswestry and into Wales

The border area to the west of Oswestry is rarely explored by visitors to Shropshire yet is delightful in many ways. It is hilly without being mountainous, has many narrow lanes to explore and offers endless opportunities for walking – Offa's Dyke Path runs north-south through it.

Although just 18 miles, this is one of the most challenging rides in the book. There are many steep hills to climb and a couple of off-road sections. However, you won't need a mountain bike – an ordinary cycle with low gears and sturdy tyres will be fine.

Do choose a clear day because for much of the ride there will be breathtaking views into the far distance. On the second off-road section, you follow part of the Ceiriog Trail to the highest point on the route at 422 metres.

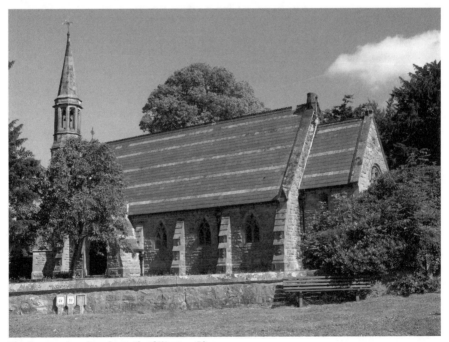

The Impressive church north of Weston Rhyn

This ride is not suitable for children because of the many hills. However, fit teenagers should enjoy it - particularly the off-road sections. Be prepared to dismount and push your cycle on the steepest parts - this is a good excuse to slow your pace and admire the views. Inevitably, there is a steady climb out of Oswestry and it's worth stopping to gather your breath and look at Old Oswestry fort, which is on the outskirts of the town. If you enjoy looking around a church, Weston Rhyn gives you another excuse to pause.

Map	Ordnance Survey 1:50,000 Landranger 126
Distance	18.5 miles (29.8km)
Waymarked	No
Gradients	Many steep hills
Surface	Asphalt and stony tracks
Shops and refreshments	Oswestry
Permits	None required

Access points

The ride starts and finishes in the centre of Oswestry - the long stay Central Car Park is handy if you arrive by car, although it is height restricted to two metres. The Horsemarket car park by the castle is not height restricted.

Oswestry has many places to eat and buy supplies. There is also a village store in Weston Rhyn but there are few other shops along the route.

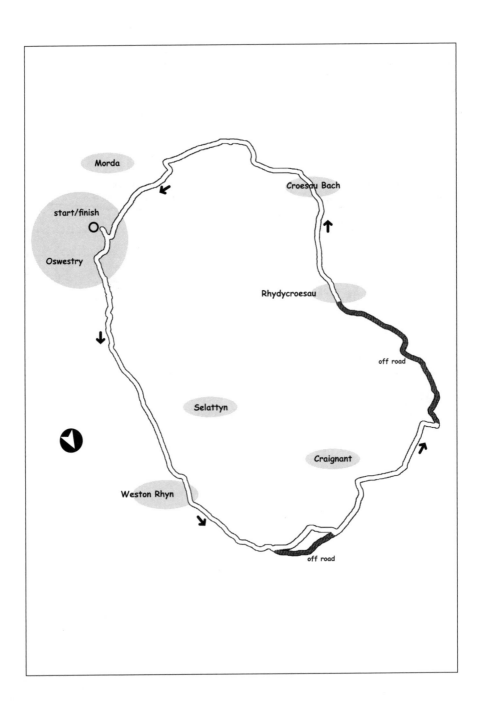

Morda

Croesau Bach

start/finish

Oswestry

Rhydycroesau

off road

Selattyn

Craignant

Weston Rhyn

off road

The route

Instruction	Miles	Comments
Turn left at road	0.00	From Oswestry Central Car Park, push your cycle out of the entrance and turn left into Salop Road
Straight @ mini-rbt		
Straight @ mini-rbt		
Straight @ x-rds		Through traffic lights then keep in left-hand lane
Follow road to left	0.45	Signposted Gobowen B5069
Left	0.50	Turn into Llwyn Road by Co-operative store. Signposted (on other side of road) Old Oswestry Hill Fort
Straight @ rbt	0.70	Begin steady ascent
	1.13	Hill fort on right at Unsuitable for coaches and HGVs sign
Left @ T	2.18	Follow blue Cycle Route 31 sign
Straight @ x-rds	2.48	Signposted Weston Rhyn. Ignore blue Cycle Route sign
Right @ T	4.23	Signposted Weston Rhyn
First exit @ mini-rbt	4.52	Signposted Quinta and Bronygarth. Village store and The Lodge public house
Straight @ x-rds	4.78	Proceed past church on right
Left	5.76	No signpost. Turn opposite a gate by a telegraph pole with a mirror. Proceed between buildings up a steep hill
Straight on where road goes left	6.01	Proceed up a steep track. Beyond Offa's Dyke Path, it is very steep and rough for about 0.5 miles and you may need to walk. Enjoy the spectacular views
		Alternatively, stay on the road and turn right after one mile to meet the end of the track

Instruction	Miles	Comments
Straight on at junction	7.10	There is a house on the right. The road to the left is where the alternative route rejoins
Left @ T	7.97	No signpost. Give way
Sharp right	8.09	Turn where signposted Selattyn and Glyn Ceiriog into unmarked road
Left	8.88	Ignore Glyn Ceiriog signpost
Right	9.87	No signpost. Join road at left bending
Left through gate	10.00	Proceed through farmyard and through a gate, then turn left immediately through another gate. Bridleway signpost
		Proceed through another gate
Fork left through gate	10.10	Signposted Llwyn Ceiriog Trail. Proceed along stony track
	10.65	Gate
Left @ x-rds	11.02	Crossroads of tracks. Proceed through gate on left between stone gateposts
	11.28	Track bends right
	11.42	Proceed through gate into Shropshire!
	12.36	Join asphalt road
Straight @ x-rds	12.79	Give way at main road. Follow sign for Pen-Y-Dyffryn Hall Country Hotel. Proceed up steep hill
Left @ x-rds	14.67	Signposted Trefonen and Oswestry. Give way
Right	15.30	No signpost. Turn by road narrows and bends ahead signs. Proceed past Unsuitable for H.G.Vs sign
Left where road bends right	15.68	No signpost. Turn opposite field gate and public footpath sign
Left @ T	16.03	Give way. Turn into Oswestry Road
Right	16.08	Signposted Morda and Maesbury
Left	16.91	Signposted Llwynymaen in Coed y go

Instruction	Miles	Comments
Right	17.04	Turn into Pen-y-llan Lane
Left	18.25	Give way. Golden Lion public house opposite
Straight at traffic lights		Past church on left
Right @ mini-rbt		
Follow road to left		
Right	18.50	Into car park

Ride 3 : Whittington north and around the Martins

Many tourists will speed north and west on the A5 trunk road as they head for North Wales unaware of the peaceful countryside they are leaving behind. Whittington, the start and finish of this ride, is just a couple of miles from the A5. However, the village and the area north of it leave the rushing traffic behind and is criss-crossed with quiet country lanes.

At just 15 miles, this is one of the shortest rides in this book and it has just one steep hill. It is mostly on roads that are rarely busy and is therefore suitable for all the family. The Shropshire Union Canal runs east-west and you cross it twice. After about five miles, the route takes you close to the border with Wales and you cross briefly into Wrexham. The wooded valley and winding river provide a pleasant

The Shropshire Union Canal – crossed twice on this ride

backdrop but there is a price to pay. To climb out of the valley, you must ascend the one steep hill on this ride. Fortunately, it only lasts for a few hundred metres so will not take long if you decide to walk rather than pedal.

Dudleston comes up next and a brief detour to view the church is recommended. Church architecture buffs will, hopefully, be fascinated by it. Those of us less knowledgeable can merely admire it as an unusual building off the beaten track.

More narrow lanes spread out ahead and with few gradients, this is easy cycling country. The views are good too even though you are no more than about 100 metres above sea level. At Hindford, you cross the Shropshire Union Canal for the second time before joining the A495, which takes you back to Whittington.

Map	Ordnance Survey 1:50,000 Landranger 126
Distance	15.0 miles (24.1km)
Waymarked	No
Gradients	One steep hill
Surface	Asphalt
Shops and refreshments	Whittington
Permits	None required

Access points

The start/finish is in Whittington, a small village with a local store and a couple of public houses. There is a car park behind the moated castle on the A495, which passes through Whittington. It is possible to cycle the two or three miles to Whittington from Oswestry – there is a shared footway/cycle path part of the way. However, this does involve crossing the A5 at a busy roundabout and so is not recommended for cycling parties with small children.

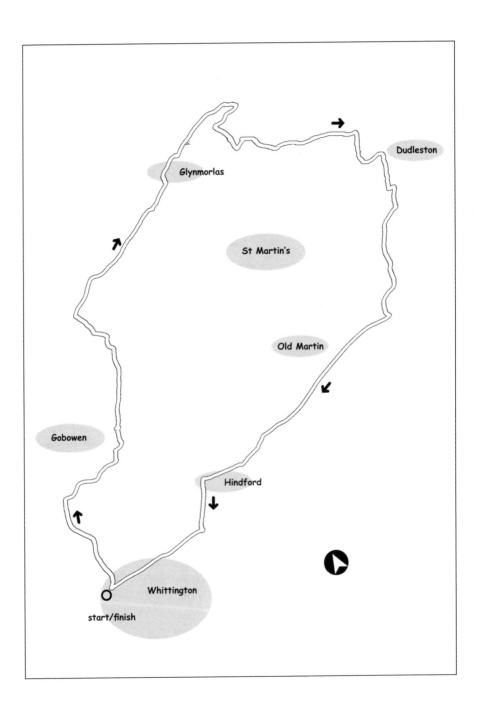

Dudleston

Glynmorlas

St Martin's

Old Martin

Gobowen

Hindford

Whittington

start/finish

32

The route

Instruction	Miles	Comments
Turn left at road	0.00	Start from the car park behind the castle and turn left at the exit
Right @ x-rds	1.20	Signposted Hindford and Ellesmere, Whitchurch Cycle Route 31
Straight on	1.92	Ignore road to Hindford signposted Cycle Route 31
Straight on	1.98	Ignore road signposted Rhosygadfa
Right @ T	3.06	Care at main road. Signposted St Martins
Left	3.13	Signposted Sarn
Straight @ x-rds	4.16	Give way at main road. Care! Signposted Glynmorlas
Right @ T	6.04	Signposted Halton
Uphill to right	6.62	After crossing bridge over river, follow road uphill (not straight on to farm). Very steep uphill for 0.5m
Left @ T	7.31	No signpost
Left @ T	7.76	No signpost
Right then left @ staggered x-rds	8.02	No signpost
Straight @ x-rds	8.52	Give way. Signposted Dudleston
	9.24	Turn left for an optional short diversion to a church with an interesting tower
Straight @ x-rds	10.34	Give way. Signposted Old Marton and Perthy
Right	11.16	Turn opposite Dudleston Hall. No signpost
Straight @ x-rds	12.13	Give way. Signposted Hindford Cycle Route 31
Left @ T	12.70	Give way. Signposted Hindford and Whittington
Left @ T	13.45	Give way. Turn by The Jack Mytton Inn. Signposted Whittington
Right @ T	14.00	Give way at main road. Signposted Whittington
Straight @ junction	15.00	By Ye Olde Boote Inn, return to car park behind castle

Ride 4 : Bishop's Castle and below The Long Mynd

A 20-mile loop around the winding lanes to the north-east of Bishop's Castle below the spectacular Long Mynd ridge. Although inevitably hilly, this ride avoids the steepest ascents yet still gives spectacular views of the Stiperstones and other hills north of Bishop's Castle. The town is also an interesting place to spend a few hours. It has some unusual shops and a choice of places for refreshments.

This is a challenging ride because of the hills to be climbed and you should allow plenty of time. It is not suitable for children. As with many of the rides which start in a town, after a short distance you are faced with a long ascent. Take it steady and enjoy the emerging views on the way up. You will reach 288 metres and, on a clear day, will have a panoramic view of South Shropshire.

A panoramic view of South Shropshire

This sets the tone for this ride – it's mostly above 200 metres and the views are endlessly changing. You pass beside The Long Mynd – a ridge that rises to over 500 metres. Walkers on the Shropshire Way or Jack Mytton Way climb it gradually but for a cyclist, the ascent is steep and best avoided. Instead, the route crosses the River East Onny valley in the sparsely populated area north-north-east of Bishop's Castle.

We do not visit The Bog on this ride (see Ride 5), although you will see it signposted, but there's a long descent down Linley Hill to enjoy. Then it's back to Bishop's Castle for welcome refreshments and perhaps a wander around the shops. After all the pedalling in a low gear, you'll be glad that the steep hill in Bishop's Castle means a descent rather than an exhausting climb to the finish of this ride.

If you want refreshments on route, it's best to take a picnic as you'll find few places to purchase food and drinks – the route passes two or three public houses only.

Map	Ordnance Survey 1:50,000 Landranger 137
Distance	20.4 miles (32.8km)
Waymarked	No
Gradients	Some steep ascents and descents but none steeper than 1 in 7
Surface	Asphalt
Shops and refreshments	Bishop's Castle
Permits	None required

Access points

The ride starts and finishes in the little car park in the centre of Bishop's Castle. It is free and there is no height restriction. This car park is well signposted from whichever direction you approach Bishop's Castle. There is also unrestricted parking on the surrounding residential streets. There are no suitable car parks along the route.

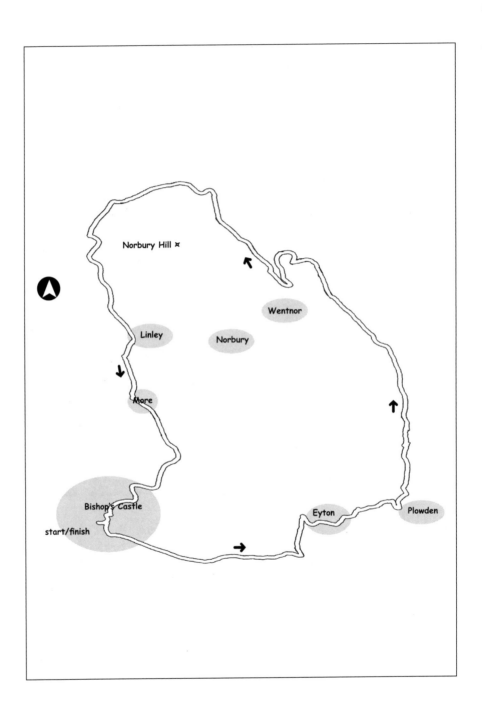

The route

Instruction	Miles	Comments
Turn right at road	0.00	Follow the signs to the small (free) car park in the centre of Bishop's Castle, just off the main street. Start from here and turn right at the exit
Right @ T	0.10	Signposted Toilets and Cattle Market
Follow road left	0.19	Signposted Clun, Craven Arms and Knighton
Straight @ x-rds	0.40	Signposted Craven Arms B4385
Straight on where road bears right	0.86	Signposted Oakeley Mynd and Five Turnings
		Steadily uphill for 1 mile, then more gradual ascent. Spectacular views
Left	2.56	No signpost. There are two gates and a small pull-in on the right
Right @ T	3.21	No signpost. Beware of downhill approach to junction
Straight on where road goes right	3.38	Signposted Eyton and Plowden
Left @ T	3.95	Signposted Plowden and Craven Arms. Join the Jack Mytton Way
Right @ T	4.51	Main road. Signposted Craven Arms and Ludlow
Sharp left	4.75	Signposted Asterton
	7.40	Proceed through Asterton
Straight @ x-rds	8.46	Give way. Signposted Adstone
	9.00	Gate! Join the Shropshire Way
	9.12	Gate! Proceed on broken asphalt track
	9.43	Gate!
Right @ T	10.16	No signpost. Give way. Beware of downhill approach
Right @ T	10.66	No signpost. Give way. Beware of downhill approach

Instruction	Miles	Comments
Left on right-hand bend	12.13	Signposted Coldhill and The Bog
Left	13.52	Signposted Linley
Left by farm	13.94	Signposted Linley. Junction easy to miss
Right @ T	16.26	Signposted More. Give way. Beware of downhill approach
Left opposite hall	16.53	No signpost. Shortcut from Ride 5 joins here.
Left @ T around church	17.25	No signpost
Left @ T	17.28	No signpost
Right @ T	17.68	Signposted Bishops Castle
Left @ T	18.22	Main road. Signposted Bishops Castle and Craven Arms
Right where road goes left	18.35	Caution! Signposted Bishops Castle B4383 and Clun
Left @ T	19.39	Signposted Clun and Bishops Castle
Right @ x-rds	19.60	Caution! Signposted Bishops Castle
Second right	20.10	Ignore the firsr right turn signposted B4385 Montgomery
		Past Three Tuns Inn and follow road left
		Down steep hill. Signposted B4385 (B4368) Craven Arms and A488 Clun
Right	20.33	Into Harley Jenkins' Street. Signposted Car Park
	20.39	Into car park

Ride 5 : North of Bishop's Castle through The Bog

At 30 miles, this is one of the longest rides in this book. However, there is a shortcut option, which reduces the distance to 14 miles. The full distance also includes some steep hills. All the exertion is worth it, however, as the area to the north of Bishop's Castle has some of the best scenery in Shropshire yet is rarely explored by visitors.

The ride takes you through The Bog – a wooded hilly area – and passes close to Stiperstones. Corndon Hill is in view for much of the ride – at 513 metres, it is one of the highest places in this area. You don't have to climb it though!

Along the way, you will pass through many small hamlets but there are few shops or public houses, except in Church Stoke (after 23 miles). You may wish to purchase supplies in Bishop's Castle and take a picnic with you – there are many places en route to stop. Bishop's Castle has a number of good places to obtain refreshments.

You will need your climbing legs and the lowest gears on your cycle for this ride. The ascending begins as soon as you leave Bishop's Castle, as you climb steadily to Bishop's Moat. It's then downhill along some narrow lanes before crossing the valley of the river Camlad.

The view from Disgwylfa Hill

Next, you follow smooth tracks around Disgwylfa Hill before climbing through a wooded area towards The Bog. A couple of sections are 1 in 7 to 1 in 5 gradient, which should encourage you to walk with your cycle and enjoy the peace and quiet.

Just off the road, Nipstone Rock is a high point of the ride at 445 metres and can be used either as an alternative starting and finishing point or as a pleasant place to stop for a picnic. Half a mile further, you can stop for teas at The Bog visitor centre – the car park opposite is another alternative start/finish point.

All that climbing has been worth it because the views to the Welsh hills in the west are spectacular and the route is now mostly downhill for a couple of miles. A short off-road section takes you across Stapeley Hill, where there are signs of much earlier inhabitants. The ground is uneven but does not call for chunky tyres or a mountain bike – just proceed cautiously.

Corndon Hill is ahead but the ride circumvents it to pass through Church Stoke and across the valley of the river Camlad again. A final steep uphill section takes you back to Bishop's Moat and then you can enjoy a long downhill run into Bishop's Castle. Do stop in the town to look at the interesting and unusual shops and to enjoy refreshments.

Map	Ordnance Survey 1:50,000 Landranger 137
Distance	29.9 miles (48.1km) or 13.8 miles (22.3km)
Waymarked	No
Gradients	Many steep hills
Surface	Asphalt and smooth track
Shops and refreshments	Bishop's Castle and Church Stoke
Permits	None required

Access points

The ride starts and finishes in the little car park in the centre of Bishop's Castle. It is free and there is no height restriction. This car park is well signposted from whichever direction you approach Bishop's Castle. There is also unrestricted parking on the surrounding residential streets. Alternative start/finish points (for the full length Ride) are Nipstone Rock and opposite The Bog visitor centre.

The route

Instruction	Miles	Comments
Turn right at road	0.00	Follow the signs to the small (free) car park in the centre of Bishop's Castle, just off the main street. Start from here and turn right at the exit
Right @ T	0.10	Signposted Toilets and Cattle Market
Right where road bends left	0.25	Signposted Bankshead, Bishops Moat and Mainstone
		Steady climb for nearly two miles with spectacular views
Left @ T	1.98	Signposted Bishops Moat and Mainstone
Right	2.46	Opposite telegraph pole D.P. 94. No signpost
Straight on where road goes left	3.64	Continue along narrow road. Ignore the track on the right
Road joins from right	3.75	Continue straight on
Left @ T	4.10	Main road, care! No signpost but mirror on pole opposite
Right	4.18	Continue downhill. No signpost
Left @ T	5.53	Main road, care!
Right	5.63	Continue uphill. No signpost
Right @ x-rds	6.76	Care! No Give Way sign or road markings
Right @ T	7.45	Main road, care!
Left	7.61	Turn where there are three metal field gates. No signpost
		Lane becomes a track
Fork right	8.09	After passing through gate
Fork right	8.29	Continue through gate and downhill
	8.51	Cattle grid
Left @ T	8.69	Cross cattle grid then give way at main road
Left	8.83	Turn where road goes downhill. No signpost but large oak tree at junction
Left @ T	9.48	No signpost

Instruction	Miles	Comments
	9.98	For shortcut, turn right beside stone wall and near large oak tree to join Ride 4
Left	10.25	Signposted Cold Hill and The Bog. Continue uphill
Fork left	10.65	Signposted Rhadley Hill and The Bog
Right @ T	11.89	Steep uphill. Signposted Bog (sic) and Stiperstones
	13.38	Parking at Nipstone Rock
Straight on	13.92	Give way. Signposted Gravels and Minsterley. Parking at Bog Mine. Toilets and teas at The Bog visitor centre
Left	14.49	Signposted Shelve and Gravels
Straight @ x-rds	16.57	Give way. Signposted Bromlow, Brockton and Worthen
Left @ x-rds	17.16	Signposted Hill Gate and Stapeley Hill
	17.57	At barrier follow track through woods
Straight on	17.74	Ignore track going left. Follow the blue waymark arrows
	18.15	Gate. Continue to follow the blue waymark arrows
Straight on	18.97	Ignore blue arrow pointing left; follow blue arrow pointing straight on. Proceed on grassy track across moorland and past a stone circle
	19.43	Cross cattle grid and proceed along gravel track
Right	19.69	Turn where track joins asphalt road. No signpost. Proceed steeply downhill, past the Old Miner's Arms public house in Priest Weston
Fork left	20.44	Signposted Churchstoke (sic) and Newtown
	21.81	Ignore fork left signposted Bishops Castle. Proceed downhill along Green Lane
Right @ T	23.09	Give way at main road. No signpost
Left	23.21	Turn before bridge. Follow road signed Unsuitable for heavy goods vehicles
Right @ T	24.52	Stop at main road. No signpost
Left	24.58	Signposted The Cwm. 2.5 miles uphill, some sections steep

Instruction	Miles	Comments
Left @ T	27.30	Signposted Bishops Castle
	27.88	Ignore turning signposted Lydbury North and proceed downhill to Bishop's Castle
Right @ T	29.42	
Right @ T	29.61	Café, restaurant and coffee shop in Bishop's Castle. Proceed down steep hill
Right	29.82	Turn at Costcutter shop
	29.90	Car park on left

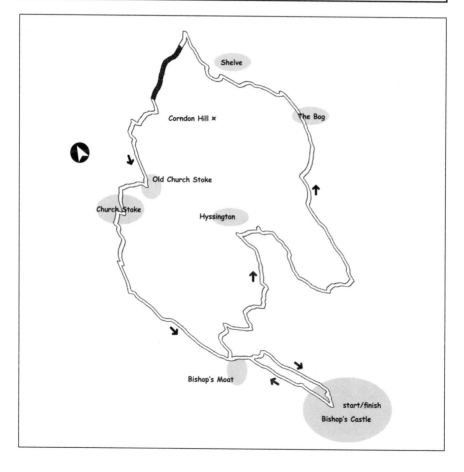

Ride 6 : A loop through the hamlets south of Ludlow

Ludlow can be accessed by car from north, south, east or west and by train from north and south. This historic town is well worth a visit and offers plenty to see, with a good choice of places to eat. It is also surrounded by some of the most attractive countryside in Shropshire – criss-crossed with quiet country lanes, ideal for cyclists. For walkers and off-road cyclists, the woods to the south-west of the town include walks and a 2km all-ability trail.

This ride explores the open countryside to the south-east of Ludlow before tackling the hills to the south-west and returning via Mortimer Forest – where you can stop for a picnic, a walk or to cycle one of the trails.

It's an undulating route with one or two steep hills and there's a short section along the busy A49 road, so is best suited to experienced cyclists. For family rides, the Mortimer Forest is recommended and this is an alternative start/finish point.

Smithfield car park was chosen as the starting point because it means you are soon out of the town and on quiet roads. You can park elsewhere or start from the railway station – make your way towards Steventon on the southern outskirts of Ludlow to pick up the route. Once you've passed under the railway line and over the A49, after just

On a hot day, you may appreciate some shade ...

more than a mile, you are on narrow country lanes. There are just a few hamlets in this area as you head south-east, parallel to Ledwyche Brook, before entering Worcestershire. Crossing the A456 and then the A49 requires care but you are soon back on quiet lanes.

This area, to the south-west of Ludlow is hilly and wooded – compared to the flat, agricultural landscape of the first eight miles of the ride. There are some steepish ascents to tackle before you pass through Elton and begin a long, stead climb to Mortimer Forest. Do allow enough time to picnic, walk and/or ride in the forest. The land on the left of the road falls away sharply and you get good views across the three rivers in this area – the Teme, Corve and Onny.

There's a welcome freewheel into Ludlow and a couple of junctions to negotiate before returning to Smithfield car park.

Map	Ordnance Survey 1:50,000 Landranger 137
Distance	19.9 miles (32.0km)
Waymarked	No
Gradients	A few steep ascents
Surface	Asphalt
Shops and refreshments	Ludlow
Permits	None required

Access points
The ride starts and finishes at Smithfield Road car park in Ludlow – which is not far from the railway station. When driving into Ludlow from either the north or south, follow signs for the free coach park. These signs can also be followed from the railway station. This pay and display car park has no height restriction and there are public conveniences beside it.

You can also park at Mortimer Forest – High Vinnalls, which is on the route and lies to the west of Ludlow. The parking area is height restricted, however. By car, Mortimer Forest is accessed from the B4361, which runs north-south through Ludlow and is, in turn, accessed from the A49, which bypasses the town.

The route

Instruction	Miles	Comments
	0.00	Turn right out of Smithfield Road car park into Sheet Road
Fork right	0.30	Proceed into Steventon New Road (do not go under the railway bridge)
	0.70	Continue uphill
Follow road left	1.26	Proceed under railway bridge and over A49. Climb steadily before going downhill
Str @ x-rds	2.34	Junction at The Serpent. Signposted Little Hereford and Tenbury
Right	3.74	Signposted Little Hereford
Right @ T	5.28	Care at main road. Signposted Brimfield and Woofferton
Left	5.44	Turn after crossing bridge. Signposted Leysters
Right	5.98	Signposted Brimfield
Left @ T	6.87	Signposted Brimfield
Right @ T	7.49	Signposted Shrewsbury and Leominster
Left	7.56	Turn by Forge House and proceed under A49. No signpost
Right @ T	7.91	Turn by Bridge Cottage. No signpost
Left @ x-rds	8.26	Care at main road. Signposted Shrewsbury and Ludlow
		Proceed past Travelodge on left
Fork left	8.46	No signpost. Proceed past Woofferton Residential Rest Home
Left @ T	10.21	Care at main road. No signpost
Right	10.31	Turn by The Castle public house. No signpost
Left @ x-rds	10.85	Signposted Goggin and Elton. Steady ascent followed by steep climb
Fork right	14.12	Signposted Ludlow
	16.33	Mortimer Forest - High Vinnalls on right. Steep ascent

Instruction	Miles	Comments
Left @ T	19.14	Care! Steep downhill approach to main road. Turn by 1 Whitcliffe Cottages. No signpost
Right	19.33	Care! Turn on left bend. Signposted Pay & Display Car Park
Left @ T	19.80	
	19.85	Turn left into car park

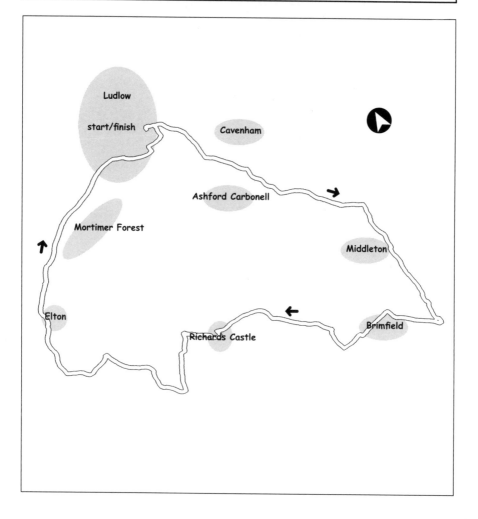

Ride 7 : South-east of Whitchurch around Shavington Park

Brown Moss is one of the most peaceful places in Shropshire

If it's a nice day and you want a picnic, this is the ideal ride. After about 20 miles, you come to Brown Moss Nature Reserve – a small wooded area with water that attracts wildfowl. Before that, the route meanders through the pleasant countryside between Whitchurch and Market Drayton and beside Shavington Park. For a longer route, you can link up with Ride 18 at Tittenley (after about 10 miles) to make a figure of eight passing through Market Drayton.

This ride starts and finishes in Whitchurch – a pleasant market town with interesting shops and a choice of places for refreshments. Cycling out of Whitchurch requires care as the roads can be busy and there are few cycle lanes or other helpful road markings. Fortunately, the bypass takes much of the traffic from the surrounding minor roads and after just a couple of miles you are in quiet country lanes. You pass through a series of small villages and agricultural countryside, with the large Cloverley Hall estate on your left. The flat landscape is liberally spotted with pools, as well as tributaries of the River Duckow, which meanders through this area.

Another country estate follows – this time the much larger Shavington Park. The ride loops around the park, returning to Ightfield where you retrace the route before turning in the direction of Brown Moss. Situated on a designated Quiet Lane, Brown Moss Nature Reserve is one of the most peaceful spots in Shropshire. You can sit among the trees, walk, watch the wildfowl and have a picnic. It's just a couple of miles back to Whitchurch – retracing the outward route through the industrial estate.

Map	Ordnance Survey 1:50,000 Landranger 117, 118, 126 & 127
Distance	23.1 miles (37.2km)
Waymarked	No
Gradients	No steep hills
Surface	Asphalt
Shops and refreshments	Whitchurch
Permits	None required

Access points

Whitchurch has several car parks close to the town centre which can be used as a start/finish point. From any of these, you need to head west for the B5398, Station Road and follow the route instructions from 0.17 miles.

The route starts at the car park beside the swimming pool and large supermarket, just off the junction between Newport Road and Bridgewater Street. On the Whitchurch bypass at the five exits roundabout which includes the A41 and A525, take the B5476 Tilstock Road towards Whitchurch. Join the B5395 and follow this into Newport Road. The car park is accessed by turning left at the next roundabout, then turning right.

You can also start from the railway station on Station Road and follow the route instructions from 0.96 miles.

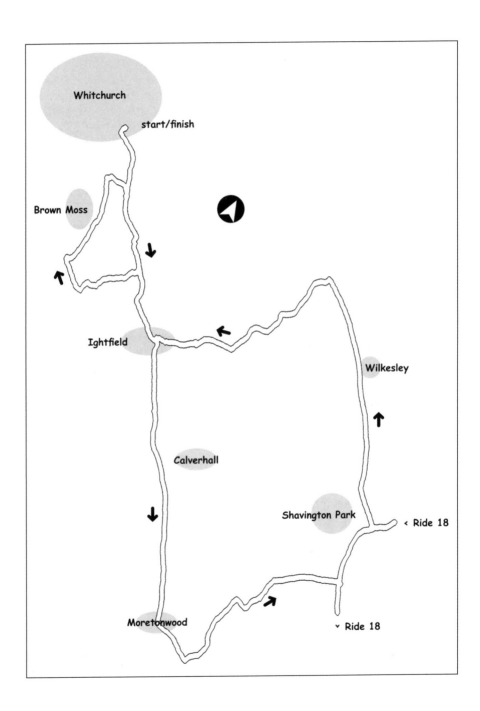

Whitchurch

start/finish

Brown Moss

Ightfield

Wilkesley

Calverhall

Shavington Park

< Ride 18

Moretonwood

ˇ Ride 18

The route

Instruction	Miles	Comments
Turn left at road	0.00	Start from the car park beside the swimming pool and supermarket, near the junction of Newport Road and Bridgewater Street and turn left at the main road. Signposted All routes
Left @ mini-rbt	0.01	Turn into Bridgewater Street. Signposted A41(N) and A49(N)
Right	0.17	Use cycle lane then turn right into Station Road at traffic lights. At this junction, there are public conveniences ahead on the left
	0.96	Railway station on left just before bridge
Cross the road	1.33	Ignore the road on the right signposted Industrial Area. Further along, cross the road onto a wide footway in front of a white bungalow
	1.37	Proceed into industrial area, using the footway (pavement) when the gate is closed (17:00 to 8:30). Continue towards roundabout
Straight @ rbt	1.49	Use footways to negotiate roundabout. Signposted Ash, Ightfield and Calverhall
		Proceed through Ash Magna and Ash Parva
Follow road left then right	4.53	Proceed through Ightfield. Signposted Market Drayton and Calverhall
	5.45	Proceed through Calverhall
Left @ x-rds	7.33	Signposted Moreton Say
Left	7.86	Turn in Moreton Say. Signposted Shavington and Adderley
Straight @ x-rds	9.50	Give way. Signposted Shavington and Adderley
Left @ T	10.35	Turn in Tittenley. Signposted Wilkesley and Audlem. Alternatively, turn right to follow Ride 18
Left @ T	11.07	Give way. Turn in Shavington. Signposted Wilkesley
Left	14.08	Signposted Ightfield
Right @ T	17.09	Give way. Turn in Ightfield. Signposted Whitchurch and Ash

Instruction	Miles	Comments
Left	18.64	Turn in Ash Parva before pond and beside The Grove. No signpost
Straight @ x-rds	19.79	Give way. Signposted Brown Moss
Right @ T	20.06	Give way. Signposted Brown Moss and Unsuitable for HGVs
	20.42	Brown Moss Nature Reserve on designated Quiet Lane
Follow road right	21.28	Signposted Whitchurch and Ash Magna
Left @ T	21.49	Give way. Signposted Whitchurch
Straight @ rbt	22.15	Use footways to negotiate roundabout
Straight	22.27	Proceed through (or around) barrier by Tension Control Bolts Ltd and then onto footway
Left @ road	22.35	Leave footway and turn left onto road
	22.73	Railway station on right
Left @ T	22.96	Turn at traffic lights
Right @ mini-rbt	23.10	Then turn right into car park to finish

Ride 8 : From Clun through Clun Forest

The title suggests a tree-lined route but Clun Forest actually has few trees these days. Instead, it is a remote and hilly area between the town of Clun and the Welsh border. The many valleys make for an undulating landscape with, on a clear day, fine views.

Clun is a small town on the River Clun with a castle and just a few shops – including a couple of good teashops. Both the Jack Mytton Way and the Shropshire Way pass through Clun and Offa's Dyke Path runs north-south just a few miles away. So, it is common to see walkers in Clun, less common to see cyclists – thanks to the hilly terrain.

However, do not be put off. This ride has some steep ascents from the word go but there is only one short section steeper than 1 in 7.

You are rewarded with excellent views on this hilly ride

The tops of the climbs are an excuse to rest and savour the views before enjoying some freewheeling.

Make sure you are carrying everything you need before starting out – including food and water. The area is sparsely populated and you pass just one public house. There are, however, many signs of ancient settlements – such as a tumulus, forts and Mottes as well as the Caerdin Ring – an Iron Age hill fort.

Map	Ordnance Survey 1:50,000 Landranger 137
Distance	17.8 miles (28.6km)
Waymarked	No
Gradients	Many steep inclines
Surface	Asphalt
Shops and refreshments	Clun
Permits	None required

Access points

There is no railway station in Clun. However, it can be accessed by car from the A488, which runs north-south, and the B4368, which runs east-west. Upon entering Clun, follow signs for the Community Area & Car Park. This is a large free car park on the north-east edge of Clun with no height restriction. If you have a vehicle to park, there are no other suitable start/finish points on the route. However, if you were feeling energetic, you could cycle from Bishop's Castle, through Colebatch and Cefn Einon to meet the Ride at Three Gates.

The route

Instruction	Miles	Comments
	0.00	Start from the car park by the Community Area and turn left to begin a long, steady climb
Keep left	1.25	Follow the road through a farmyard. Enjoy panoramic views
Right @ T	2.00	Care at steep downhill approach to main road. No signpost
Left	2.47	Signposted Bicton
Right	3.02	Signposted Three Gates and Mainstone. More ascents and good views
Left	4.17	Signposted Three Gates and Two Crosses. More ascents
		Proceed across x-rds in Three Gates. Cross Offa's Dyke Path. Proceed across x-rds at summit
Left	7.57	Turn where there are pine trees on the left. If you come to a five-way junction, you have gone too far! No signpost. Proceed downhill
Right @ T	10.19	Care at downhill approach to junction. No signpost
Right @ T	10.84	Care at downhill approach to junction. Give way. No signpost
Left @ x-rds	11.46	Junction in Newcastle. Signposted Clun and Craven Arms. Proceed to cross river
Right	11.82	Turn on uphill left bend. Care! No signpost. Steep ascent for 1 mile
Left @ x-rds	12.84	Junction in Stoney Pound. Signposted Springhill and Clun
Left @ x-rds	15.43	Give way. Signposted Clun. Proceed downhill
Left @ T	17.05	Give way. Signposted Clun
Right	17.15	Care! Turn by church. No signpost
		Proceed downhill (steep) and through ford (or use footbridge). Proceed uphill to the right
Left @ T then right	17.51	Give way. Turn right by chapel. No signposts
Right @ T	17.67	Signposted Clun Community Area & Car Park
	17.75	Turn left into car park

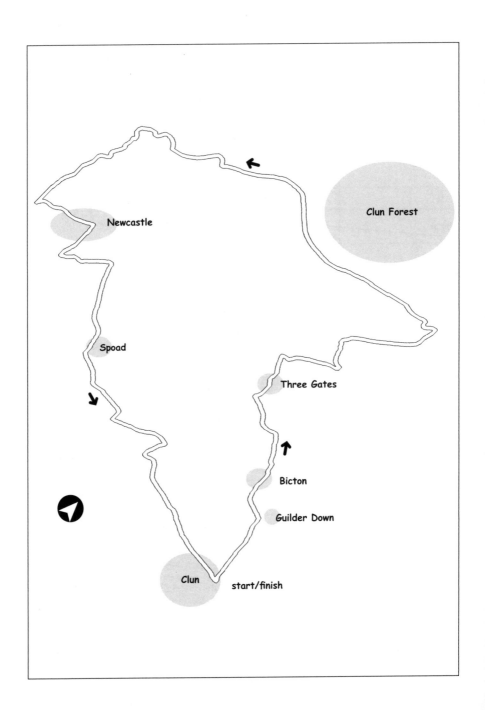

Ride 9 : Circuit of the Meres

The Meres around Ellesmere offer excellent scenery and attract lots of wildlife. Some, such as Sweet Mere, are quite small while The Mere, at Ellesmere, is the largest and most popular with tourists. This seven-mile route is a short family ride which starts and finishes at Colemere Countryside Heritage Site – an enjoyable place to picnic and spend some time. Ride 10 starts and finishes at the same place and the two rides can be combined to form a 30-mile figure of eight.

Waymarked Regional Cycle Network routes 31 and 38 in this area can be followed if you wish to venture further afield.

You begin by passing through the village of Lyneal – following cycle route 31. There's a short section on the B5063 before you rejoin quiet country roads through mainly agricultural scenery. You are now in Wales and cross the Shropshire Union Canal before following the national boundary for a little way. After cycling through Breaden Heath, you come to Welshampton where you can pause for refreshments (there's a village shop and a public house) or admire the impressive church. You cross the canal once more before returning to Colemere Countryside Heritage Site.

Map	Ordnance Survey 1:50,000 Landranger 126
Distance	7.30 miles (11.7km)
Waymarked	No
Gradients	No steep inclines
Surface	Asphalt
Shops and refreshments	Ellesmere
Permits	None required

Access points

The start/finish point is Colemere Countryside Heritage Site, where there is plenty of parking space. The site, which is a couple of miles south-east of Ellesmere, is easily reached from north or south along the A528. Whitchurch is about 10 miles away on the A495.

The route crosses the popular Shropshire Union Canal

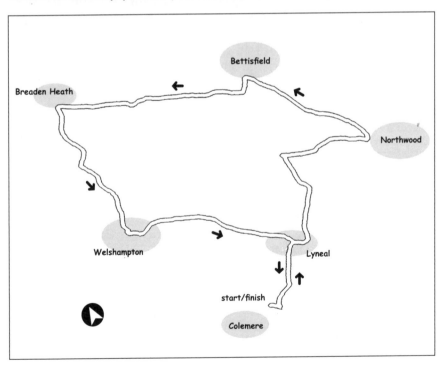

The route

Instruction	Miles	Comments
	0.00	Turn left out of Colemere Countryside Heritage Site
Right @ T	0.60	Signposted Loppington and Wem
Left @ T	0.78	Signposted Balmer Heath and Wem, also Cycle Route 31
Right @ T	1.63	Give way. Signposted Northwood and Wem, also Cycle Route 31
Left	2.35	Turn after entering 30mph limit. Signposted Bettisfield
Left	3.52	Turn before entering Bettisfield. Signposted Breaden Heath. Cross canal
Right @ T	4.34	No signpost
Right & left @ staggered x-rds	4.64	Care! Signposted Breaden Heath, Hampton Wood and Penley
Left	5.21	No signpost. Turn opposite Public Footpath sign
Left @ T	5.86	No signpost
Right @ x-rds	6.40	Signposted Welshampton and Stocks
Left @ T	6.56	No signpost
Left @ T	6.61	Give way. No signpost. Church opposite
Right	6.65	Care! Turn alongside church. Signposted Lyneal and Cycle route 31
Right @ T	6.67	Junction in Lyneal. Give way. Signposted Colemere and Ellesmere
Left	6.70	Signposted Colemere
	7.30	Colemere Countryside Heritage Site on right

Ride 10 : Criss-crossing canals around Ellesmere

Just south-west of Ellesmere, the Shropshire Union canal is joined by the Montgomery branch of the canal. In the same area, there are a number of quiet country lanes. The result is many canal bridges – which invariably offer good views of the generally flat landscape. There is also the prospect of seeing narrow boats and swans on the canals plus other wildlife attracted to the water.

This ride is 22 miles and has only one notable incline. It is suitable for a pleasant family ride one afternoon or can be linked with Ride 9 to form a longer figure of eight route. The ride passes close to Ellesmere where you can stop for refreshments. The start and finish point at Colemere Countryside Heritage Site is an ideal place to picnic and there is a pleasant picnic area just past Lower Frankton.

Quiet lanes abound in Shropshire

You begin by looping around Cole Mere, crossing the canal twice before passing through Spunhill, with White Mere on your left. At about six miles, you pass close to the marina in Ellesmere. This is an excellent place to stop if you want to watch people messing about in boats!

Another canal crossing follows after Tetchill, before you briefly join the A495. You can pause at the church in Welsh Frankton – its elevated position commands excellent views. Now you swoop down through Lower Frankton – crossing the Shropshire Union Canal at the junction with the Montgomery Canal. Another canal bridge follows – possibly the most humped in Shropshire. A picnic spot on the left is a good place to pause and could be an alternative start/finish point.

Passing through Tetchill again, the route continues on winding country lanes and leaving the canal behind. There's a village shop and a public house in Cockshutt if you want refreshments.

Map	Ordnance Survey 1:50,000 Landranger 126
Distance	22.5 miles (36.2km)
Waymarked	No
Gradients	One long, steady climb
Surface	Asphalt
Shops and refreshments	Ellesmere
Permits	None required

Access points

As with Ride 9, the start/finish point is Colemere Countryside Heritage Site, where there is plenty of parking space. The site, which is a couple of miles south-east of Ellesmere, is easily reached from north or south along the A528. Whitchurch is about 10 miles away on the A495.

You could also complete the ride from the car park and picnic site beside the canal just south of Lower Frankton. Turn off the A495 Whittington-Ellesmere road at Welsh Frankton and pass through Lower Frankton. The car park is just after a very humped bridge.

The route

Instruction	Miles	Comments
	0.00	Turn left out of Colemere Countryside Heritage Site
Left @ T	0.60	Signposted Newton and Ellesmere
		Cross canal
Left @ x-rds	1.73	No signpost. Weight limit 10 tonnes 1/2 mile ahead sign.
		Cross canal
Right @ x-rds	2.59	Junction in Colemere. Signposted Spunhill and Ellesmere
Straight @ x-rds	3.65	Junction in Spunhill. Give way. Signposted Lee
Right @ T	4.61	Give way. Signposted Ellesmere
Left @ T	5.78	Signposted Tetchill and Queens Head. Canal bridge on right
Right	7.15	Junction in Tetchill. Turn where road bends left. Signposted Welsh Frankton
Left	7.50	Turn after crossing canal. No signpost. Long steady climb
Left @ T	8.80	Give way and care! Signposted Whittington
Left	8.87	Signposted Lower Frankton
		Cross canal and then cross canal again over a very humped bridge. Parking area with picnic tables on left
Left @ T	11.11	Give way. No signpost
Fork left	11.35	Signposted Hordley, Tetchill and Ellesmere
Right	12.78	Turn in Tetchill by Rose Cottage into Farm Lane. No signpost. Pass between 30mph signs
Right @ T	12.91	No signpost
Left @ T	14.66	No signpost
Right	14.90	Signposted Kenwick Park and Cockshutt. Road signed as Unsuitable for long vehicles
Follow road left	15.74	In Kenwick Park, signposted Cockshutt

Instruction	Miles	Comments
Left @ T	17.76	Turn in Cockshutt. Give way. Signposted Ellesmere
Right	17.81	Care! Signposted English Frankton and Loppington. Village shop in Cockshutt
Left	19.23	Signposted Pikesend (sic) and Colemere
Left @ T	19.41	No signpost
Right	20.39	Past Pikes End farm, turn right at bridge over stream. No signpost
Left @ x-rds	21.71	Junction in Lyneal. Turn opposite road signposted Loppington
Left @ T	21.81	Give way. No signpost
Left	21.92	Signposted Colemere
	22.50	Colemere Countryside Heritage Site on right

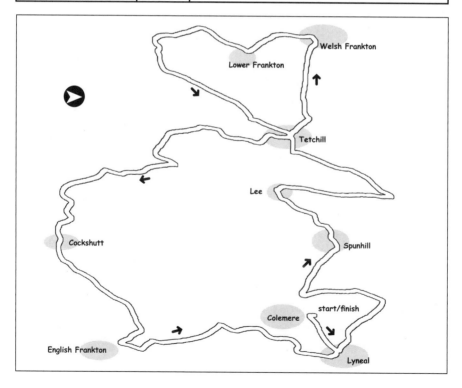

Ride 11 : From Wem to Whixall Moss

Shropshire is rightly famous for its mosses – mostly concentrated in North Shropshire District. Ride 7 takes you past Brown Moss, which is a nature reserve. This route explores the area north of the market town of Wem, which includes many mosses. Their presence indicates mostly flat countryside – which is lightly populated and largely unspoilt. Ideal for cycling, in other words. If you want to explore a moss, Whixall Moss (another nature reserve) is on the route (7 miles from the start) and there is a 1.75-mile Orange Trail around it. It's an area abundant with wildlife.

At 15 miles and with no significant ascents, this ride is ideal for a family day out. There are no main roads to cross and just 0.5 miles on a B road. The short off-road section is not demanding. For the more adventurous, by turning left after five miles and cycling through Northwood, you can add the 7-mile loop of Ride 9.

The route takes you alongside the Shropshire Union Canal

Wem is an excellent start and finish point. It has a railway station and can be accessed by B roads from all points of the compass. As a small market town, it has a wide selection of shops and a number of places for refreshments.

You are soon out into the countryside – heading towards Dobson's Bridge where you cross the Prees Branch of the Shropshire Union Canal. Next, you cross the Shropshire Union Canal and cycle beside it for a little way. This is Whixall Moss and there are two or three car parks, which could be alternative start/finish points. After re-crossing the canal, the route proceeds through the maze of winding lanes around Whixall. There are no hills to speak off and little traffic so it is pleasant cycling. After linking up with Regional Cycle Route 38, you return to Wem.

Map	Ordnance Survey 1:50,000 Landranger 126
Distance	15.2 miles (24.5km)
Waymarked	No
Gradients	No steep inclines
Surface	Asphalt, grass and gravel
Shops and refreshments	Wem
Permits	None required

Access points

Wem railway station is the start and finish point. It is situated on the B5065 a little way from the town centre and there are direction signs to it in Wem. There is a small, free, car park with no height restriction. For public conveniences, turn at the White Lion public house in the centre of Wem (0.5 miles from the station) and they are on the right. They are closed from 18:00 to 8:00.

You could also park at or near Whixall Moss and start and finish the ride from there. Whixall Moss is best reached from the A495 Whitchurch-Ellesmere road. Head through Fenn's Bank towards Whixall and then follow the signs to Whixall Moss National Nature Reserve.

The route

Instruction	Miles	Comments
	0.00	Exit the railway station car park straight across into Station Road
Straight @ x-rds	0.42	Proceed into Pyms Road. Signposted Swimming Pool and Butler Sports Centre
Right @ T	0.88	Turn at the end of Pyms Road. No signpost
Left @ T	1.81	Signposted Loppington and Whixall
Right	2.24	Turn where road bends left. Signposted Newtown
Right	3.76	Turn where road bends left by the Church of King Charles the Martyr. No signpost
Right @ T	5.00	Give way. No signpost. Turn left to and then right in Northwood to join Ride 9
Left	5.90	Turn by a house with white posts in the verge. Road marked as dead end. No signpost. Proceed to cross canal
Right @ T	6.32	No signpost
Left @ T	6.41	Give way. No signpost
Left	6.58	Signposted Whixall Moss
Right	6.95	At canal bridge (Morris's Bridge no. 45), cross the canal and immediately turn right to proceed on towpath - which is uneven but not rough
	7.43	Follow towpath beneath bridge and proceed to join track
Follow track to left	7.73	
Right @ T	8.06	Continue on another track and proceed to join asphalt road
Right @ T	8.58	Give way. Brown sign Whixall Moss - NNR
Straight @ x-rds	8.83	Give way. Signposted Hollinwood and Tilstock
Right	9.33	Turn in Hollinwood opposite what appears to be a derelict chapel. No signpost
Right	9.92	Turn in Stanley Green. No signpost
Straight @ mini-rbt	9.95	Signposted Bostock Hall

Instruction	Miles	Comments
Right @ T	10.71	Give way. Signposted Bostock Hall and Ellesmere
Left	10.81	Signposted Braynes Hall
Left @ T	11.66	Junction in Abbey Green. Give way. Signposted Edstaston and Waterloo
Left @ T	12.20	Signposted Edstaston
Right @ T	12.83	Give way. No signpost
Right @ T	14.23	Give way at main road and proceed on B5476. No signpost
Left	14.80	Turn into Summerfield Road by Hawkestone Arms public house on right
	15.16	Railway station car park ahead

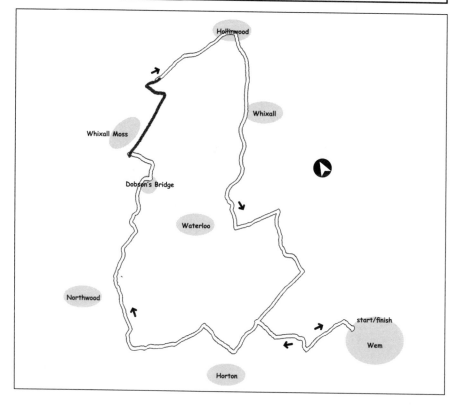

Ride 12 : A loop from Haughmond Hill

Haughmond Hill is a wooded area of Forestry Commission land on the eastern outskirts of Shrewsbury. It's an excellent place to walk and have a picnic. You can also visit the nearby Haughmond Abbey.

To the south is a low-lying area in the wide plains of the River Severn and Cound Brook valleys. Thanks to a bridge across the busy A5 trunk road, this area is accessible from Haughmond Hill and offers easy cycling along quiet country lanes. The ride takes you past Attingham Hall stately home and deer park, past Wroxeter Roman City and through the memorably named hamlet of Cound Stank!

It's quite long at nearly 27 miles but there are no significant ascents. Part of it is off road – along a relatively smooth track. It is suitable for a family ride, with just one short section along a B road.

Heading south from Haughmond Hill, you join National Cycle Route

In Atcham, you turn onto the old bridge over the River Severn

45 briefly before crossing the A5. With Attingham Park on your left, you come to a tricky junction in Atcham. You want to cross the main road and then turn right onto an old road to cross the River Severn on the old bridge. The route then criss-crosses Cound Brook – first at a ford. I make no excuses for including many fords in these rides – crossing them on a cycle is much more fun than in a vehicle!

Passing quickly through Cound Stank, there's then another main road junction to negotiate at Cressage. You cross the River Severn again before joining a quiet lane to proceed through the tiny hamlet of Eyton on Severn. Wroxeter Roman City follows before an unpromising looking turning ahead of an industrial estate – marked as a no through road. Sure enough, the road narrows to a track and becomes impassable for vehicles but not cyclists (or horses). Pause on the bridge over the River Tern and watch the traffic rushing past on the A5. If you've brought some bread, you could feed the swans. It's now just a couple of miles to Haughmond Hill, with a steady climb to finish the ride.

Map	Ordnance Survey 1:50,000 Landranger 126
Distance	26.8 miles (43.1km)
Waymarked	No
Gradients	No steep hills
Surface	Asphalt, grass and gravel
Shops and refreshments	Shrewsbury
Permits	None required

Access points

Haughmond Hill is signposted from the B5062 east of Shrewsbury and there is free parking with no height restriction. It is open dawn until dusk. You could also cycle from Shrewsbury railway station – although the roads can be busy at times. National Cycle Network routes 45 and 81 pass close to Haughmond Hill if you want to venture further afield. Wroxeter Roman City beside the B4380 near Wroxeter is on the route and has a free car park with no height restriction.

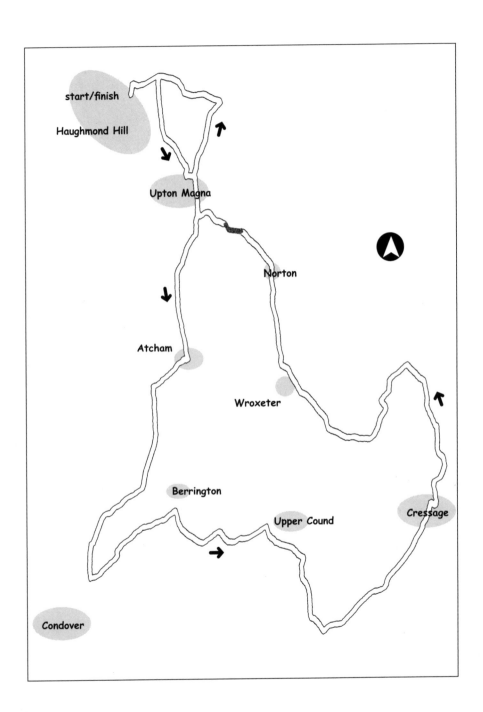

The route

Instruction	Miles	Comments
	0.00	Exit Haughmond Hill and turn right
Right @ x-rds	0.48	Signposted Upton Magna and Atcham
Left @ T	1.84	Junction in Upton Magna. Signposted Rodington, Atcham and Wellington
Right @ T	2.02	Turn in front of The Corbet Arms. Signposted Berwick Wharf and Atcham. Join Cycle Route 45
Left @ T	3.40	Give way. Signposted Atcham. Proceed on Cycle Route 45
Straight @ x-rds then right	4.29	Give way and cross main road to turn right onto old bridge
Left @ T then right	4.43	Turn onto road at end of bridge and then turn right almost immediately into road signed Unsuitable for heavy goods vehicles
Straight @ x-rds	5.01	Care and give way at main road. Signposted Condover
Straight @ x-rds	6.43	Give way. Signposted Condover
Left	7.85	Signposted Boreton (Through Ford). Proceed through ford but be warned that it may be deep and slippery. Alternatively, use the footbridge
Straight @ x-rds	8.94	Signposted Berrington and Cross Houses
Right	9.55	Junction in Berrington. Signposted Eaton Mascott
Right @ T	11.37	Junction in Cound Stank. Signposted Pitchford and Acton Burnell
Left	11.46	Signposted Upper Cound and Cressage
Left	13.27	Signposted Cressage
Right @ T	15.74	Care and give way at main road. Turn onto Shrewsbury Road
Left	15.80	Turn into Station Road. Signposted Telford B4380

Instruction	Miles	Comments
Straight @ x-rds	17.07	Care and give way at main road. Signposted Eaton Constantine, Uppington and Wellington
Sharp left	17.43	Turn on right bend. No signpost. Proceed past church on right
Left @ x-rds	17.91	Signposted Eyton on Severn and Shrewsbury. Join Cycle Route 45
Straight @ x-rds	18.35	Care and give way at main road. Signposted Dryton and Eyton on Severn
Straight @ x-rds	21.39	Care and give way at main road. No signpost. Proceed along road signed 7.5T except for access. Wroxeter Roman City on right
Straight @ x-rds	21.91	Care and give way at main road. Signposted Allscott B4394 and Walcot
Left	22.02	Marked as a no through road. No signpost
	23.00	Cross river on narrow bridge and join track (not rough)
Left	23.15	Turn where track meets asphalt lane
Right @ T	23.74	No signpost. Proceed on bridge over A5 trunk road and through Upton Magna
Fork left	24.55	Signposted Rodington and Roden
Left @ x-rds	25.16	Signposted Haughmond Hill and Shrewsbury
Straight @ x-rds	26.35	Give way. No signpost
	26.84	Turn into Haughmond Hill

Ride 13 : From Ironbridge around The Wrekin

Ironbridge, a World Heritage Site, is the site of the famous Iron Bridge. There are ten museums to visit as well as Blists Hill Victorian Town. The Wrekin, on the other hand, is a legendary hill and a familiar landmark in Shropshire. From the top of it, you can see 15 counties. This ride links Ironbridge and the Wrekin in a 16-mile loop along narrow lanes and on two off-road sections. It starts with a long ascent out of Ironbridge and part of one of the tracks used can be badly rutted so this is best described as a challenging ride.

You won't pass many shops along the route, although there are a few public houses. It's probably best to pack a picnic and enjoy it on The Wrekin. You get good views all along this ride but for the best vantage point, you will need to walk from the road to the top of The Wrekin – which is 400 metres above sea level.

The famous Iron Bridge

For a longer ride, you can use National Cycle Network route 45 to link up with Ride 16. Cross the Iron Bridge heading away from the town and then turn left onto route 45.

As the start is near the River Severn in Ironbridge, it is inevitable that there's a climb to begin the ride. Although never steep, it is relentlessly uphill for the first mile and a half. You then join the first off-road section and pass beside a quarry and into a farmyard. The next off-road section takes you down Maddock Hill and within site of The Wrekin. You can walk to the top from the first car park you come to or continue pedalling around the base of The Wrekin. Although the area is popular with tourists, few venture along the narrow lanes south of The Wrekin. Little Wenlock is the highest point of the route and it is mostly downhill to Ironbridge and the finish. Do pause often to admire the industrial landscape and don't forget to walk with your cycle across the Iron Bridge.

Map	Ordnance Survey 1:50,000 Landranger 127
Distance	15.6 miles (25.1km)
Waymarked	No
Gradients	Some steep ascents and descents
Surface	Asphalt, grass and gravel
Shops and refreshments	Ironbridge
Permits	None required

Access points

There are two car parks in Ironbridge from which you could start and finish this ride. Each is on the right-hand side as you enter Ironbridge from the A4169, past the power station. Dale End Car Park is the first you come to and the better choice. There is no height restriction and at the time of writing, it cost £1.40 to park for more than two hours. There are, however, no toilets. Wharfage car park is a little further towards Ironbridge centre and does have toilets. Again, there is no height restriction but the maximum stay is three hours – barely enough time for this ride.

National Cycle Network Route 45 runs through Ironbridge beside the river on the south side. Cross the river at the Iron Bridge to join it.

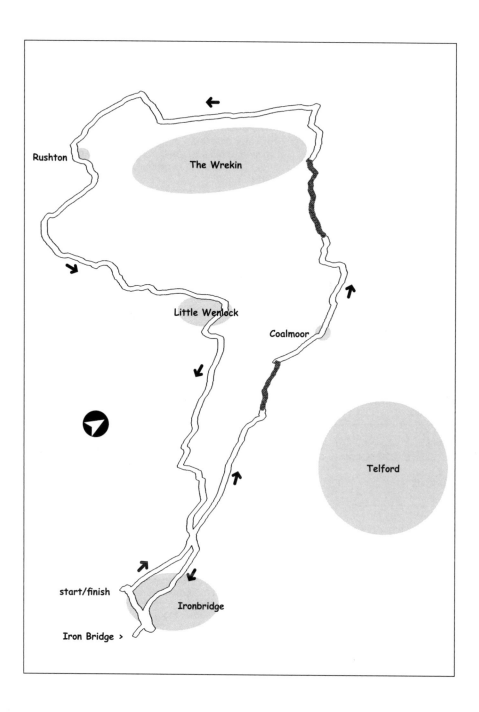

Rushton

The Wrekin

Little Wenlock

Coalmoor

Telford

start/finish

Ironbridge

Iron Bridge >

The route

Instruction	Miles	Comments
	0.00	Exit Dale End Car Park and turn right (left from Wharfage Car Park)
Left @ mini-rbt	0.01	Turn into Dale Road. Signposted Museum of Iron. Proceed uphill past Coalbrookdale Museum. Pass under railway bridge and continue uphill for a further 1 mile
Left before rbt	1.73	Approaching Jiggers Roundabout, turn left onto a bridleway to run parallel to the road. The road is signposted Ironbridge, Much Wenlock and A4169
Cross road	1.80	Cross the A4169 and along a bridleway heading up the embankment (to the right of a lay-by). Proceed onto a grassy track beside a perimeter fence and then pass a farm on the left and go into a muddy yard
Left through gate	2.37	In the yard, proceed through the gate to the left onto an asphalt road
Right @ T	2.40	Lower Coalmoor Farm is on the left. Proceed past Badger Cottage on the right. No signpost
Right @ T then left	2.73	Signposted Candles Works
Left @ T	3.43	Signposted Huntington
Right	3.60	No signpost. After 0.25 miles, the road becomes a track. Continue uphill towards trees in the distance
Fork left	4.31	Ignore the track on the right leading through a metal gate and proceed downhill to the left. Care! Steep descent on track badly rutted in places
Right @ T	4.69	Join asphalt road. No signpost
Left	5.05	Turn where road bends right. Signposted Shrewsbury
Left	5.23	Signposted Uppington and Eaton Constantine
Left @ x-rds	6.96	Signposted Eaton Constantine and Cressage
Left @ x-rds	7.51	Junction in Rushton. Signposted Nevers Castle and Little Wenlock
Left	8.41	Junction in Nevers Castle. Signposted Leighton and Little Wenlock

Instruction	Miles	Comments
Right @ T	10.73	Junction in Little Wenlock. Signposted Horsehay and Dawley
Right	10.90	Turn opposite The Hunstman public house into Church Lane
Right @ T	11.27	Signposted Coalbrookdale and Ironbridge
Right	13.00	Turn into Darby Road just before passing under railway bridge. Proceed alongside bridge
Follow road left	13.25	Pass through bridge arch. Beware of speed bumps. Pass the Museum of Iron
Straight @ x-rds	13.51	Give way. Signposted Old Vicarage Guest House. Proceed steeply uphill for 0.5 miles
Right then right @ T	14.02	Junction by The White Horse public house. Join main road
Fork left	14.14	Proceed into Church Hill
3rd exit @ rbt	14.59	Junction at bottom of hill
	14.70	Iron Bridge on left. Cross it and turn left to follow cycle route 45 to join with Ride 16
	15.59	Turn left into car park

Ride 14 : From Church Stretton below Wenlock Edge

Wenlock Edge and The Longmynd are two of the most famous ridges in Shropshire. Church Stretton lies between them and is consequently popular with walkers. However, for all but the most energetic cyclists, each ridge offers daunting ascents. Ride 4 explores the area below and to the west of The Longmynd and this ride does a similar thing with Wenlock Edge. The result is excellent views of the ridge, without the need to climb it!

Although the busy A49 runs north-south through Church Stretton, most of the minor roads in this area are perfectly suited to cycling. Church Stretton is an excellent start/finish point as it has a wide choice of teashops along with other interesting places to visit. Indeed, you won't pass many shops or public houses en route so Church

A cyclist may be the object of curiosity

Stretton is the place to stock up with provisions – and food for a picnic.

This is one of the longer rides and you should allow sufficient time to complete it. It is also necessary to cross the A49 road twice, so the route is not suitable for young cyclists.

From the start, you head south along the valley floor through Little Stretton before crossing the A49 at Marshbrook. Narrow roads take you to the base of Wenlock Edge and then run more or less parallel to it. Much of Wenlock Edge is wooded, whereas the area below it is agricultural land – mostly for grazing.

There are several tiny hamlets in this area and just a few villages large enough to warrant a church – such as Rushbury and then Cardington. A gentle ascent out of Cardington is followed by a short, steep descent before a junction with the A49. At certain times of the day and of the year, this can be a busy road so be cautious as you cross it to head towards All Stretton and then the finish.

Map	Ordnance Survey 1:50,000 Landranger 137
Distance	20.7 miles (33.3km)
Waymarked	No
Gradients	Hilly with one or two steep ascents
Surface	Asphalt
Shops and refreshments	Church Stretton
Permits	None required

Access points

You can get to Church Stretton on the A49 from Shrewsbury to the north or Ludlow to the south. The town also has a railway station. Easthope Road Car Park is a convenient place to start and finish. There is no height restriction and there are toilets in one corner. At the time of writing, the charges were £2.40 for up to four hours and £3.60 for up to 10 hours.

To reach the car park, turn towards Church Stretton town centre from the A49. The railway station is on the left. Easthope Road Car Park is signposted on the left, just past the railway station.

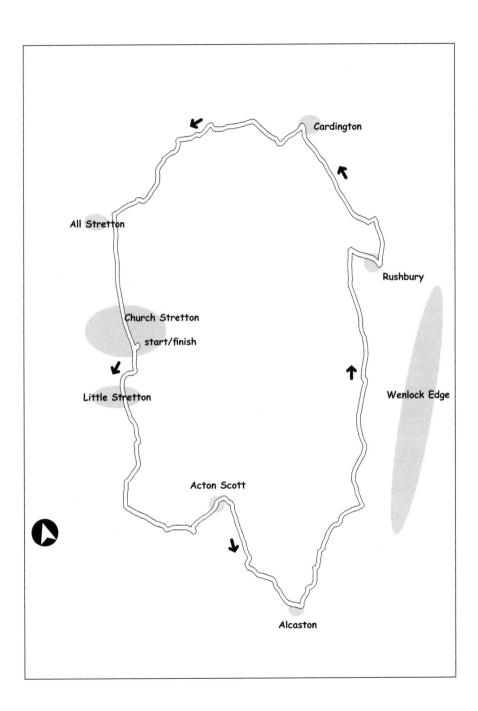

Cardington

All Stretton

Rushbury

Church Stretton

start/finish

Wenlock Edge

Little Stretton

Acton Scott

Alcaston

The route

Instruction	Miles	Comments
	0.00	Exit Easthope Road Car Park facing the Co-op store and turn right. Turn left at the mini-rbt by the Bucks Head public house
Right @ x-rds	1.54	Turn by The Ragleth Inn. No signpost. Proceed to follow the road to the left
Fork right	1.70	Pass between speed de-restriction signs. No signpost
Left @ x-rds	2.79	Junction in Minton. Signposted Marshbrook
Left @ T	3.71	Care! Steep downhill approach to main road. Give way. Turn by The Station Inn and proceed over the level crossing
Right @ T	3.73	Give way at main road. Signposted Leominster A49
Left	3.91	Signposted Acton Scott and Ticklerton. Proceed steeply uphill
Right @ x-rds	4.60	Junction in Acton Scott. Signposted Henley
Fork left	5.60	Signposted Henley and Alcaston
Straight on	6.60	Junction in Alcaston. Give way. Signposted Wolverton and Harton
Left @ T	8.58	Signposted Eaton and Ticklerton
Right	8.96	Junction on left bend. Signposted Eaton
Left @ T then right	10.36	Pass between bridge supports then turn right. Signposted Wall
Right	12.13	Turn before junction with main road. Signposted Rushbury and Beambridge
Left	12.63	Junction in Rushbury. Signposted Longville and Much Wenlock
Left @ x-rds	13.21	Give way at main road. Signposted Hope Bowdler and Church Stretton
Right	13.34	Care! Junction on left bend. Signposted Gretton and Cardington. Proceed along Gilberries Lane
Left @ x-rds	14.95	Signposted Cardington and Leebotwood

Instruction	Miles	Comments
	15.46	Proceed through Cardington, signposted Leebotwood and Church Stretton
Left	17.26	Junction (easy to miss) in Comley. Turn just before road goes right. Signposted Botvyle and Church Stretton
Left then right	18.44	Care! Give way at main road. Not signposted. Proceed down road signed Unsuitable for heavy goods vehicles
Left @ T	18.90	No signpost
	20.57	In Church Stretton, proceed into High Street
Left @ mini-rbt	20.64	Junction by Bucks Head public house
	20.72	Turn left into car park

Ride 15 : From Bridgnorth towards the highest point in Shropshire

At 540 metres, Abdon Burf, on Brown Clee Hill, is the highest point in Shropshire. Unsurprisingly, the views from the top are extensive and it is a place well worth visiting. Abdon Burf is surrounded by country lanes, small hamlets and agricultural land. This makes cycling to Abdon Burf a pleasant experience – especially as it doesn't involve steep hills, just steady climbing. The nearest road takes you to Brown Clee Picnic Site at 320 metres – from where you can see for many miles on a clear day. This is, obviously, an ideal place to pause for a picnic. To reach the summit means walking 200 metres higher.

Because Bridgnorth is an interesting historic town to the east of Abdon Burf, it makes an ideal start/finish point. At just over 22 miles, this is another of the longer routes in the book. However, as you weave your way toward Abdon Burf on winding lanes, the miles roll by easily. Then, having savoured the view from the highest point, there's the prospect of a mostly downhill ride back to Bridgnorth.

You enjoy good views of the agricultural landscape

Bridgnorth is not an easy town to cycle out of without using main roads. By starting at the Severn Valley Railway car park, you can at least be on quiet country lanes after only three miles or so. They are, indeed, very quiet country lanes, joining many small, scattered hamlets. You climb steadily as you pass through Tedstill, Oldfield and Wrickton – crossing a number of brooks and their tributaries. The ascents get a bit steeper as you approach the high point of the Ride but only one short section has a 1 in 7 gradient. As you would expect, the views from Brown Clee Picnic Site are splendid and, on a clear day, extensive.

You head down through Ditton Priors – losing altitude remorselessly but still enjoying spectacular views of the countryside. There's a couple of short sections on B roads before you're back at the car park.

Map	Ordnance Survey 1:50,000 Landranger 138
Distance	22.3 miles (35.9km)
Waymarked	No
Gradients	Hilly with one or two steep ascents
Surface	Asphalt
Shops and refreshments	Bridgnorth
Permits	None required

Access points

Although there are a number of car parks in Bridgnorth, the best one to start and finish this ride at is the car park for the Severn Valley Railway. It is well signposted in Bridgnorth, has no height restriction and gives access to the route without using busy roads. At the time of writing, it cost £2 per day to park. There are no toilets at the car park though. On weekends when steam trains are running on the Severn Valley Railway, the car park gets full and you will be directed to an overflow car park a few hundred metres away.

Bridgnorth is crossed by the A458 and A442 and can be accessed easily by road from Shrewsbury, Wolverhampton, Stourbridge and Kidderminster.

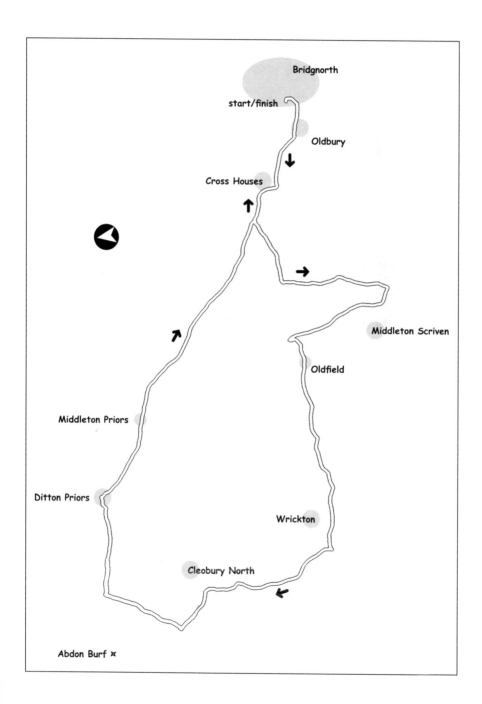

Bridgnorth

start/finish

Oldbury

Cross Houses

Middleton Scriven

Oldfield

Middleton Priors

Ditton Priors

Wrickton

Cleobury North

Abdon Burf ✗

The route

Instruction	Miles	Comments
	0.00	Exit Severn Valley Railway car park and turn right. Proceed past Jewson store on the right
Right	0.15	Care! Signposted Cleobury B4363. Proceed for 0.75 miles uphill
Right	0.80	Junction in Oldbury, just past church on right. Proceed into Manor Farm Lane
Right @ T	1.61	No signpost
Left @ T	1.84	Give way at main road. Signposted Ludlow B4364
Left	3.35	Signposted Deuxhill, Middleton Scriven and Eudon George
Right	5.22	Signposted Middleton Scriven
Right @ T	7.26	Signposted Oldfield
Left @ T	7.81	Junction in Winterburn Bridge. Signposted Walkerslow, Neenton and Burwarton
Right @ T	9.91	Junction in The Baytree. Signposted Cleobury North and Ditton Priors
Straight @ x-rds	11.47	Give way. Signposted Ditton Priors
Left	11.88	Follow road left signposted Ditton Priors then turn left signposted Abdon and Tugford
	12.70	Brown Clee Picnic Site
Right	13.27	Turn just past telephone kiosk. Signposted Ditton Priors and Bridgnorth
Left @ T	13.89	Give way. Signposted Ditton Priors
Right @ x-rds	14.31	Turn by church. Signposted Middleton Priors, Lower Netchwood, Brown Clee School, Village Hall
Left @ T	20.09	Care and give way at main road. No signpost. Proceed to cross river
Right	20.50	Care! Signposted Kinlet and Cleobury Mortimer
Left	20.73	This junction is easy to miss. No signpost
Left @ T	21.53	Give way. Turn opposite Oldbury Lodge. No signposted
Left @ T	22.13	Give way. Signposted Shrewsbury (A458)
	22.28	Turn left into Severn Valley Railway car park

Ride 16 : Shifnal to Blists Hill and back

Telford may seem an unlikely location for a ride in the country but this route proves it is possible. Indeed, there are sections of the route where there are few signs of civilization. From the countryside south of Shifnal, the Ride takes you along the Silkin Way towards Ironbridge – with its many museums – and past the Blists Hill Victorian Town. You return along cycle tracks through Telford Town Park to the starting point in Shifnal.

This route is just over 15 miles and because much of it is away from traffic, it makes a good family ride – with just one steep ascent to Nedge Hill and a couple of short off-road sections.

If you want a longer, more challenging ride that loops to the south of Telford, divert from the Silkin Way to join with Ride 13 starting in Ironbridge.

The route includes a couple of off-road sections

From the starting point in Shifnal, there's just a little distance to cycle along the A464 before you divert on to country roads. After a gentle rise to the top of Brimstree Hill, there's an equally gentle descent before the route winds through Grindle. The off-road section that follows takes you across the intriguingly named Mad Brook. Another off-road section links to the stop of a steep hill above the River Severn and you then join cycle tracks.

Paralleling the River Severn at first, the cycle track then winds north through the suburbs of Telford towards the Town Park and the town centre. However, this route leaves the cycle track to proceed through Stirchley and on up the short, steep Nedge Hill. You could pause for a picnic here before proceeding downhill to join A roads to the finish.

Map	Ordnance Survey 1:50,000 Landranger 127
Distance	15.3 miles (24.6km)
Waymarked	No
Gradients	One steep hill
Surface	Asphalt, grass and gravel
Shops and refreshments	Shifnal and Blists Hill
Permits	None required

Access points

Shifnal is just a few miles from junction 4 of the M54, on the outskirts of Telford. It also has a railway station – turn left at the bottom of the hill for the start/finish car park. This free car park (not height restricted) is signposted in Shifnal if you are travelling by car. You could also use Blists Hill as a start/finish point.

Although only a small town, Shifnal has a good selection of shops and places to get refreshments.

The route

Instruction	Miles	Comments
	0.00	Exit the car park in Shifnal and turn right
Left @ T	0.12	Proceed under railway bridge
Right	0.41	Turn on left bend. Signposted Grindle, Kemberton and Ryton
Right @ T	3.22	Signposted Kemberton and Madeley
Left	3.32	Turn just past Grindle Cottage. No signpost
Straight @ x-rds	3.67	Give way. Proceed onto bridleway. This is a wide, uneven track. Proceed through ford or use footbridge
Right @ T	4.24	Give way. Join asphalt road
Left	4.47	Turn where there are old iron fences on sides of road. No signpost
Straight @ x-rds	4.86	Give way at main road. Signposted Sutton Maddock
Right @ T then left	5.63	Give way. Signposted Sutton Hall Farm. This is a wide, uneven track
Fork left	5.91	Ignore Sutton Hall Private Road
Right	6.56	Turn just proceed past scrapyard on left onto track that is generally smooth but potholed in places
Left	6.88	Give way and proceed onto asphalt road. No signpost
Right	7.10	Immediately after crossing Coalport Railway Bridge and before Weak Bridge, turn right onto Silkin Way
	8.54	Turn right for Blists Hill Victorian Town. Otherwise, continue on Silkin Way, following signs for National Cycle Network route 55
	9.77	Cross railway on bridge and go underneath road. Follow route 55 for Town Centre
Right	11.01	Turn at sign Welcome to Telford Town Park and concrete bench inscribed Rest After Work
Right	11.22	Turn onto asphalt cycle track by Fletcher's Pool
Right @ T	11.33	Proceed downhill on cycle track
Right	11.42	Turn at houses
Left @ T	11.54	Join asphalt road

Instruction	Miles	Comments
Left @ T	11.68	Turn into Grange Avenue. Signposted Telford Town Centre and Randley
Right at mini-rbt	11.79	Proceed along Randley Avenue
Right @ T	12.14	Turn into Stirchley Avenue
Left	12.21	Turn by The Nedge Tavern. Signposted Nedge Hill. Keep left to proceed into Nedge Lane. Proceed steeply uphill to Nedge Hill Picnic Site, then downhill
Left @ T	14.39	Give way at main road. No signpost
Left @ rbt	14.65	
4th exit @ rbt	14.91	Signposted Town Centre
Left then right	15.17	Pass between HSBC and Barclays banks
	15.25	Left into car park or continue for railway station on right

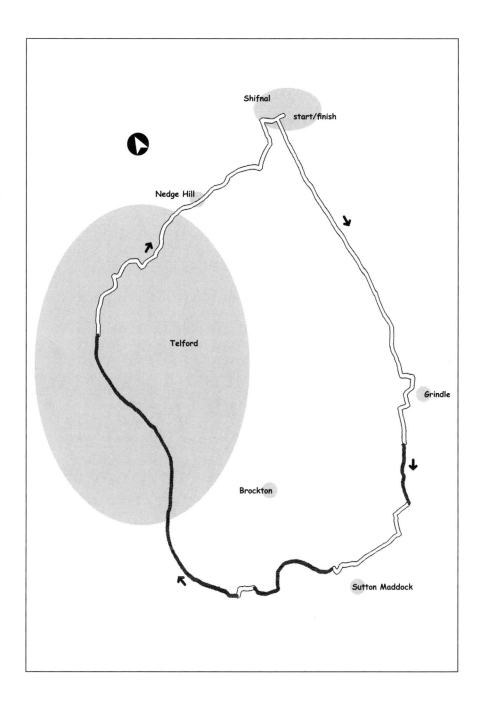

Ride 17 : Newport to Granville Country Park

If you think all of Shropshire is hilly, this Ride will change your mind. It rolls gently through the countryside to the north-east of Telford, which is criss-crossed with rivers and streams. It is true that you do not get the far-reaching views of some of the hillier rides but compensation comes in the form of pleasant agricultural scenery.

The roads used are generally quiet and winding and there are two long off-road, traffic-free, stretches. These can be tackled easily on an ordinary touring or commuter cycle so, thanks also to a lack of steep ascents, this makes for an excellent family ride. Beware of the short section of busy roads after around 14 miles and at 23 miles. The route is quite long so allow plenty of time.

Heading west from Newport, you are soon on relatively quiet roads.

Look out for the splendid old trees in Shropshire

This is a low-lying, sparsely populated area with mainly straight and level roads. The River Meese meanders through this area together with the River Strine and its many tributaries. After Kynnersley, the first off-road section takes you alongside a dead straight ditch before you turn onto a dead straight track. There are some busy roundabouts to negotiate before you skirt Muxton and proceed along tracks near Granville Country Park. You join the road again near the remains of Lilleshall Abbey and pass through Lilleshall before crossing the A518 to return to Newport.

Map	Ordnance Survey 1:50,000 Landranger 127
Distance	23.0 miles (37.0km)
Waymarked	No
Gradients	No steep hills
Surface	Asphalt, grass and gravel
Shops and refreshments	Newport
Permits	None required

Access points
Newport is just a few miles from Telford and the M54 so, despite its lack of railway station, is a convenient starting point. The ride goes past Granville Country Park on the outskirts of Telford so you could start/finish there – and cut out the loop into Newport.

Although it is only a small town, Newport has a good variety of shops in the main street and a choice of places to get refreshments. There are several car parks in Newport. New Street car park is just off the main street, is free and has no height restriction. There are, however, no public toilets. If you use a different car park, cycle to the main street through Newport town centre and start the ride opposite St Nicholas Church, heading north-west (there's a weather vane on the church).

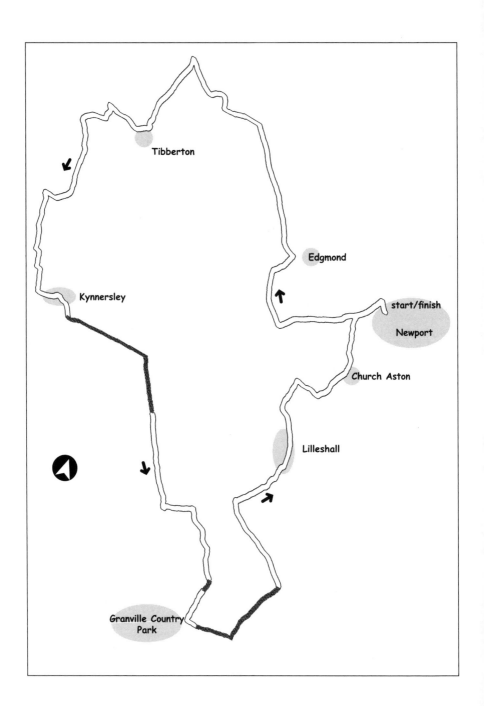

Tibberton

Edgmond

Kynnersley

start/finish

Newport

Church Aston

Lilleshall

Granville Country
Park

The route

Instruction	Miles	Comments
	0.00	Exit the New Street car park and proceed left. Dismount and push your cycle through the short one-way section. Turn left and start the ride opposite St Nicholas Church facing north-west (towards a Shell filling station)
Left @ mini-rbt	0.22	Turn into Salters Lane
	0.55	Continue into Longford Road
Right @ T	1.75	No signpost
Left	2.74	Make the turn past a church on the left and opposite playing fields on the right. No signpost. Continue into Hillside
Straight @ x-rds	3.44	Give way. No signpost. Proceed past Harper Adams University College
Left @ T	5.73	Signposted Tibberton and Great Bolas
Right @ T	6.76	Junction in Tibberton. Signposted Cherrington and Kinnersley (sic)
Left @ T	7.44	Signposted Kinnersley (sic) and Crudington
Straight @ x-rds	8.29	Give way. Signposted Kynnersley and Preston
Fork left	11.10	Turn onto track just before passing through speed limit de-restriction signs. No signpost. Proceed onto bridleway
Right	12.41	Turn where bridleway ends onto muddy lane. There is a house at the junction. Join an asphalt road after 0.75 miles
2nd exit @ rbt	13.55	Proceed into Station Road. Signposted Muxton and Donnington
2nd exit @ rbt	14.10	Signposted Muxton
Straight @ mini-rbt	14.20	
Left	14.33	Turn into Wellington Road. Signposted White House Hotel & Restaurant
Right	14.82	Turn into Muxton Lane. Signposted The Shropshire Open Golf and Leisure Comlpex (sic). Continue uphill and past the Granville Country Park sign on the right. Follow the road to the right in front of some houses and proceed along a (short) uneven track

Instruction	Miles	Comments
Right @ T	15.94	Turn where the track meets an asphalt access road
Left @ T	16.31	Turn just after crossing a cattle grid and opposite a 'beware of horses' sign. No signpost. Continue along a potholed track and ignore a right fork
Left	16.98	Turn before passing through a metal gate. Proceed along another track with a hedge each side
Left @ T	17.90	Join asphalt road. No signpost
Right	19.09	Turn at 30mph speed limit signs into Church Road
Straight @ rbt	20.29	Signposted Brockton and Edgmond
Right	20.75	Turn at left bend. Care! Signposted Church Aston and Newport
Left @ T	21.36	No signpost
Left @ T	21.43	No signpost
Left	21.89	Signposted Vauxhall
Right @ T	22.55	No signpost. Proceed into Longford Road and then Salters Lane
Right @ mini-rbt	22.97	Turn opposite The Swan public house
	23.00	St Nicholas Church. Return to car park

Ride 18 : A northern loop from Market Drayton

The area north of Market Drayton is mostly flat and scenic and has the Shropshire Union Canal running through. Thanks to main roads running both north-south (the A529) and east-west (A53), the lanes in this area are relatively traffic free.

This relatively short ride includes just 0.5 miles along the A529 and has no significant gradients. It is, therefore, ideal for a family ride. If you feel more adventurous, you can link with Ride 7 for a 36-mile figure of eight.

Market Drayton offers a number of places for refreshments but has no railway station. You can start from any of the car parks in the town. As you head out of Market Drayton, you cross the A53, with its fast-moving vehicles, and the Shropshire Union Canal, with its much slower traffic. This is a cue to join quiet country lanes around Betton and heading towards Adderley. The area is quite flat and dotted with many pools. Be careful on the short stretch of the busy A529 – especially at the right turn on the left bend at six miles.

You can now join Ride 7 or continue south towards Market Drayton along the valley of the River Duckow. By proceeding through Longford, the route passes beneath the A53 to enter Market Drayton on residential roads. You can now follow cycle route signs back to the town centre.

Map	Ordnance Survey 1:50,000 Landranger 127
Distance	13.0 miles (20.9km)
Waymarked	No
Gradients	No steep hills
Surface	Asphalt
Shops and refreshments	Market Drayton
Permits	None required

Access points

There is no railway station in Market Drayton. By car, you can reach Market Drayton from Shrewsbury along the A53 and from junction 3 of the M54 on the A41.

Park where you can in Market Drayton (there are several car parks) and make your way to the Tourist Information Office in Cheshire Street. You need to be heading north-west (as if going to Nantwich) to begin the ride. There are no suitable car parks along the route.

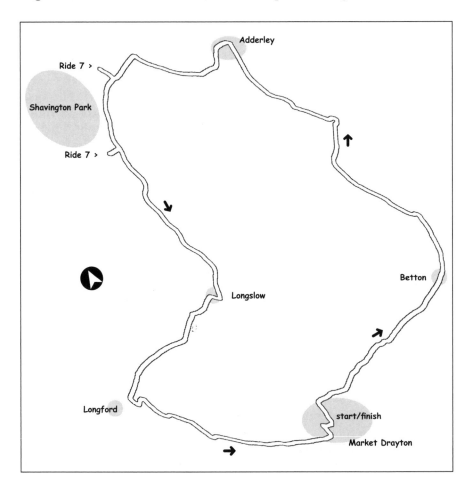

The route

Instruction	Miles	Comments
	0.00	Leave the Tourist Information Office in Cheshire Street on your left and proceed north-west as if heading for Nantwich
Right @ mini-rbt	0.31	Turn right by Morrisons into Maer Lane, signposted Maer Lane Industrial Estate. There are toilets by this roundabout. Proceed to cross the A53 and the Shropshire Union Canal
Left	2.40	Turn after Betton Hall. Signposted Ridgwardine and Adderley
Left @ T	4.16	Signposted Adderley and Audlem. Proceed to cross the Shropshire Union Canal again
Left @ x-rds	5.42	Turn in Adderley. Signposted Market Drayton
Left @ T	5.57	Care! Give way at main road. Signposted Market Drayton. You may prefer to cross the road and use the footway around the bends and past the church. Care when re-crossing road
Right	5.98	Care! Where roads bends left, turn right. Signposted Shavington and Wilkesley
Left	6.94	Turn left where road goes right in Shavington. Signposted Spoonley. Alternatively, continue right to follow Ride 7
Right @ T	9.13	Signposted Longslow and Calverhall
Left @ T	9.13	Signposted Market Drayton
Right	9.63	Turn where road bears left. Signposted Longford
Left @ T	10.77	Give way. Signposted Market Drayton plus blue Cycle Route sign
Left @ T	11.67	Give way. Signposted Town Centre on blue Cycle Route sign. Cross road to use cycle lane, then turn right between barriers and continue following blue signs
Left @ T	11.81	Follow blue sign
Left @ T	11.86	Follow blue sign
Right @ T	11.90	Follow blue sign
	13.00	Finish in town centre

Market Drayton has many fine old buildings

Ride 19 : From Craven Arms along a Roman Road

Not the prettiest of towns, Craven Arms nevertheless makes an ideal starting point for cycle rides. It has a railway station and is accessed easily by car. It is surrounded by beautiful countryside and myriad quiet lanes. Craven Arms has many shops and places to eat and the Discovery Centre, just south of the town, is well worth visiting.

Although quite short, this is a hilly ride and you should be prepared to walk up some of the ascents. It is worth doing so to enjoy the views across the valleys and the wooded slopes.

From the starting point at the railway station, you head west on the road to Clun but soon turn to join a Roman road – of which there are few in Shropshire.

Look out for the splendid old trees in Shropshire

As you would expect, it is quite straight but it is certainly not level and you ascend remorselessly to Shelderton in the shadow of Shelderton Hill.

You leave the straight and narrow behind, to join winding but still narrow lanes plus a particularly steep (but short) hill approaching Aldon. This is followed by a sweeping descent to the River Onny. At Onibury, you cross the busy A49, the railway line and the river to climb out of the valley and reach a high point at Norton. It's down and up again to Lower Dinchope before the final run into Craven Arms.

Map	Ordnance Survey 1:50,000 Landranger 137
Distance	15.1 miles (24.3km)
Waymarked	No
Gradients	Hilly with some steep ascents
Surface	Asphalt
Shops and refreshments	Craven Arms
Permits	None required

Access points

The car park beside the railway station in Craven Arms is the start/finish point. It is free but has a 10' 0" height restriction. There are no toilets at the car park but there are some soon after starting the ride.

Craven Arms is on the busy A49 road, which runs north-south and can be accessed easily from Shrewsbury or Ludlow. There are east-west routes passing through Craven Arms too.

There are no other obvious start/finish points for this route.

The route

Instruction	Miles	Comments
	0.00	Leave the car park by the railway station and proceed into Station Crescent
Right @ T	0.10	Give way. Toilets on left by bus stop
Right @ rbt	0.37	Signposted Clun B4368. Proceed beneath railway bridge
Left	0.98	Signposted Rowton and Shelderton. Proceed under railway bridge along Roman Road. Steady climb for one mile
Left	4.35	Turn after crossing small bridge over stream and passing post box on right. No signpost. Proceed uphill and follow signpost for Onibury and Ludlow. Continue up long, steep hill
Fork left	5.46	Signposted Brandhill
Left	6.01	Turn by telephone kiosk. Signposted Brandhill
Follow road right	6.72	Turn at white house on left. No signpost. Proceed steeply downhill, through sharp bends then steeply uphill
Right @ T	8.16	No signpost
Left @ X-rds	9.39	Give way. No signpost
Left @ T	9.43	Give way and care joining A49. Signposted Shrewsbury and Craven Arms
Right	9.58	Turn just after level crossing. Busy road, care! Signposted Walton and Norton
Left	9.64	Turn in front of The Apple Tree Free House. Signposted Norton
Straight @ x-rds	11.98	Give way at main road. Signposted Upper Dinchope and Lower Dinchope
Left	13.01	Signposted Halford, Strefford and Craven Arms
Left @ T	13.15	Signposted Halford, Strefford and Craven Arms
Left @ T	14.23	Give way. Signposted Craven Arms

Instruction	Miles	Comments
Right @ T	14.43	Give way. Signposted Craven Arms
Right @ mini-rbt	14.88	
Left	15.06	Signposted Station
	15.13	Proceed into station car park

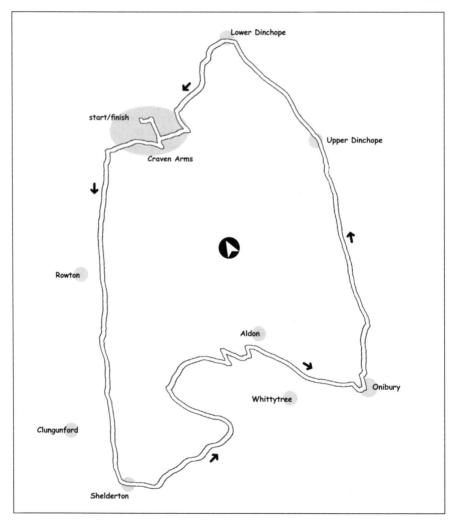

Ride 20 : From Ludlow along Corve Dale

Being accessible easily by car and train, the historic and interesting town of Ludlow is a good place to start and finish a cycle ride. Ride 6 explored the area to the south of the town, this route takes you north-east, along Corve Dale and parallel to Wenlock Edge – but on the other side to Ride 14. The route passes through many ancient hamlets as it climbs to 270 metres before an undulating descent (via California) into Ludlow.

This 24-mile ride is not for the fainthearted but the effort is worth it for the magnificent views across to Wenlock Edge. If you wish to avoid the steepest climbs, there is a shorter route option which trims the total distance by about five miles.

You start from the same place in Ludlow as Ride 6 but head north out of the town (passing the railway station) and cross the A49 via a bridge. Be sure to follow the road around to the left at the junction after the bridge over the A49 – the return route is the turn off that goes straight ahead. With the wide valley of the Corve Dale to your left, you continue to follow the road as you pass a succession of hamlets – Lower Hayton, Little Sutton, Great Sutton and so on. So far, it's a gently ascending ride on quiet lanes through a mainly agricultural landscape.

In Bouldon, you need to decide whether to complete the full 24 miles or opt for a shortcut. On the longer route, the ascents get steeper but with spectacular far-reaching views as compensation. The shortcut is less steep.

Earnstrey is the high point of the ride at around 270 metres but to the east, the land rises higher still – to Abdon Burf. This is the highest point in Shropshire at 540 metres and is the destination of Ride 15. If you want to divert to the Brown Clee Picnic Site, turn towards Hillside and follow the road around the hill.

It is now downhill most of the way. This time the hamlets you pass through are Abdon, Cleemarsh (where the shortcut joins) and Clee St Margaret. There's a ford at Clee St Margaret, which is potentially hazardous, but exhilarating to pedal through.

Follow the road for about another six miles and you're back at the junction mentioned above – so you now retrace the route to the starting point.

Ludlow is famous for its traditional shops

Map	Ordnance Survey 1:50,000 Landranger 137
Distance	24.0 miles (38.6km) with 19.0 miles (30.6km) option
Waymarked	No
Gradients	Steep ascents and long climbs
Surface	Asphalt
Shops and refreshments	Ludlow
Permits	None required

Access points
The ride starts and finishes at Smithfield Road car park in Ludlow. When driving into Ludlow from either the north or south, follow signs for the free coach park. This pay and display car park has no height restriction and there are public conveniences beside it. The route passes the railway station – turn left after exiting the station to continue from the second instruction below.

There are no other obvious start/finish points for this route.

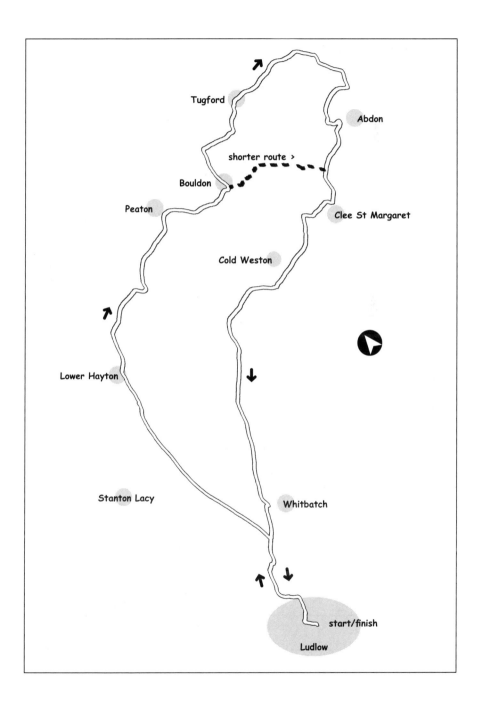

Tugford

Abdon

shorter route >

Bouldon

Peaton

Clee St Margaret

Cold Weston

Lower Hayton

Stanton Lacy

Whitbatch

start/finish

Ludlow

The route

Instruction	Miles	Comments
	0.00	Turn left out of Smithfield Road car park. Follow the road to the right in front of Somerfield. Pass the exit from the railway station
Left @ T	0.65	Sign on left to hospital
Right	0.90	Turn into Fishmore Road before passing under the railway bridge
		Ignore all left and right turns for several miles
Straight on where road goes left	7.94	Junction in Peaton. Signposted Bouldon and Heath
Left	8.97	Signposted Tugford and Holdgate. Alternatively, for shorter route, follow road to right, signposted Heath and Cockshutford
Right @ T	9.66	No signpost
Right	10.73	Take the second right in Tugford. No signpost. Proceed past Tugford Farm B & B. Long, steady climb with good views
Right @ T	12.38	No signpost. More climbing
Right @ T	13.06	Signposted Abdon and Tugford
Left @ T	13.83	Signposted Clee St Margaret and Ludlow
Straight @ x-rds	14.94	If following shorter route, turn right @ x-rds and deduct 5 miles from distances. Signposted Clee St Margaret and Ludlow
Right	15.59	Proceed through ford - care, may be slippery. Signposted Ludlow
Left @ T	22.01	Give way. Signposted Ludlow
Left @ T	23.00	Signposted Kidderminster and Bridgnorth
Right	23.28	Turn opposite Post Office. Signposted Free coach park. Proceed past road to railway station
	24.00	Turn into car park

Ride 21 : A circular route from Pontesbury

The south-west of the county, running along the wide valley of the Rea Brook from Shrewsbury to the Welsh border, is often overlooked in terms of the beauty of the landscape – except for the Stiperstones ridge which is rightly popular with walkers. For cyclists prepared for some steep climbs and lengthy ascents, the quiet roads running each side of the valley offer peace, quiet and wonderful views.

The start and finish point chosen is handy for those travelling by car with their cycles but it would be equally possible to ride out from Shrewsbury along the A488. A glance at the Ordnance Survey map for this route will reveal plenty of black arrows indicating steep gradients. Certainly, a lot of climbing is involved – steep uphill sections and long, steady ascents. The exertion is well worth it because of the stunning views from the high points. Of course, for every ascent, there's a descent and towards the end of the ride, you are rewarded with a four-mile freewheel into Westbury.

After climbing and descending in the largely wooded area to the south of Pontesbury, you arrive in Minsterley and depart along the valley floor. The route then heads into the maze of quiet lanes on the southern edge of the valley with Hope in mind! Having reached an altitude of 380 metres, the route takes you to the valley floor once more at Brockton (not to be confused with the village of the same name near Much Wenlock).

Climbing out of the valley through Hampton Beech, the route passes near the Grade II* listed Hampton Hall built in the 17th century. Reaching the highest point on the ride at 389 metres you join a Roman Road and can enjoy a welcome freewheel for a few miles. The ruins of Caus Castle – once a border stronghold – are nearby as you enter Westbury. With the toughest part of the route behind you, it's perhaps time to admire the interesting architecture in Asterley – most of which is designated a conservation area. There are a number of listed buildings in the village and a 12th century church – St Mary's. After cycling through Pontesbury, there's just one final climb to the finish – although if you have the energy you can walk to the summit of Earl's Hill at 320 metres.

Map	Ordnance Survey 1:50,000 Landranger 126
Distance	24.6 miles (39.6km)
Waymarked	No
Gradients	Steep ascents and long climbs
Surface	Asphalt
Shops and refreshments	Pontesbury, Minsterley
Permits	None required

Access points

This ride starts and finishes at Earl's Hill nature reserve, which is owned by the Shropshire Wildlife Trust and where there is a small car park. The A488 Shrewsbury to Bishop's Castle road runs through Pontesbury. Just north-west of the town, a turning off the A488 is indicated with a brown sign for Earls Hill Nature Reserve and Pontesford Hill. Follow the narrow lane steeply uphill and turn left into the nature reserve car park.

Alternatively, you can start and finish at Eastridge Woods south of Pontesbury. Along the A488, turn at MInsterley towards Habberley. Turn right at the T-junction, bear right at the fork and take the next right up a narrow lane. There are marked off-road cycle trails in Eastridge Woods. If starting here, follow the route below from instruction five.

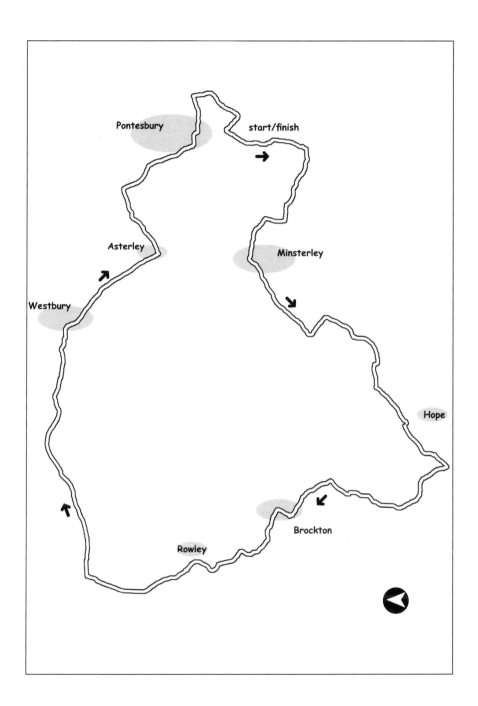

The route

Instruction	Miles	Comments
	0.00	Turn left out of Earl's Hill nature reserve car park
Right	0.45	Follow the road round to the right and downhill
Left @ T	0.75	Turn left at the end of Grove Lane. The road goes steadily uphill. Enjoy the views
Right	2.00	Right at timber-framed house. Signposted Minsterley. Steep uphill
	2.35	Eastridge Woods - alternative start/finish
		The road goes steeply uphill and then steeply downhill
Left @ T	3.95	In Minsterley
Right @ rbt	4.00	Signposted Westbury B4387 etc
		Cross a bridge over a stream and proceed past a Post Office
Left @ rbt	4.10	Signposted Worthen B4499 and National Cycle Route 44
Left	5.40	Take a left turn on a right-hand bend just past Ferndale Farm. Not signposted. Look for a road sign warning of cattle just after turning
Right @ T	5.85	Not signposted
		Steadily uphill
	6.90	Uphill and downhill with more steady climbing
Straight @ x-rds	7.90	Signposted Bentlawnt, Hemford
		More uphill. Continue past Post Office
Straight @ x-rds	8.35	Signposted Hemford, Bromlow
		More uphill!
Right @ x-rds	8.75	Signposted Bromlow, Brockton
		At 380 metres, this is the second highest point on the route
Straight on	9.42	Give way at junction by The Callow Inn. Signposted Bromlow, Brockton

Instruction	Miles	Comments
		Steep downhill
Straight on	9.80	Straight on at junction joining National Cycle Route 44
Left @ T	10.90	Signposted Brockton, Worthen. Care on B-road
Right @ T	11.75	Signposted Shrewsbury B4386 etc
Left	11.80	Turn immediately after crossing bridge. Signposted Hampton, Rowley
	12.64	Continue towards Hampton and Rowley, steep uphill
Straight @ x-rds	13.85	Signposted Vennington, Vron Gate
	14.70	More climbing to 389 metres - the highest point on the route
Right @ T	15.67	Signposted Vennington, Westbury
		Downhill virtually at the way to Westbury - nearly four miles!
Right @ T	19.10	Signposted Minsterley, Worthen
Right @ T	19.30	Not signposted
Straight @ x-rds	19.33	Signposted Asterley, Pontesbury. Proceed on to Hinwood Road
Left	21.10	Turn in Asterley before a T-junction. Not signposted. After turning pass Church House Farm on right
Right	22.20	Turn by Farley House. Signposted Pontesbury
Left @ x-rds	23.46	Signposted A488 Shrewsbury. Turn into one-way street
		Continue out of Pontesbury in direction of Shrewsbury, past the Nags Head public house
Right	24.25	Care! Signposted Poentesford Hill, Earls Hill Nature Reserve. This is the final climb!
	24.60	Finish at Earl's Hill nature reserve car park on left

Ride 22 : Shrewsbury loop

Shrewsbury was chosen to receive Connect2 funding from Sustrans, the sustainable transport charity. As a result, some new cycle routes and cycle crossings have been opened in the town with more planned or under construction at the time of writing.

This Shrewsbury loop starts and finished alongside the River Severn near The Quarry (see below for alternative start/finish points), uses traffic-free routes to exit Shrewsbury to the east before looping around the south of the town on quiet lanes. There are a few climbs to tackle but the reward is a long downhill run almost into Shrewsbury to the finish. Other rewards include fabulous views across the River Severn valley and pleasant cycling along the country lanes in the Atcham district.

Running alongside the River Severn, the first part of the route is level and traffic free – although (especially on sunny days) watch out for pedestrians, wayward toddlers and dogs! After cycling through Ditherington, it's back to a traffic-free bridleway that doubles as the Shropshire Way – a circular walk around the county. The sadly neglected Shrewsbury & Newport canal is your neighbour for a while further along this canal at Longdon on Tern, north-east of Shrewsbury, Thomas Telford built the first cast iron aqueduct.

Leaving the Old Shrewsbury Canal Countryside Heritage Site, the route continues on quiet country lanes through successive villages before reaching Atcham. Here is one of the three busy arterial roads out of Shrewsbury that you'll cross on this ride. Cautious riders may well choose to dismount and push their cycles across the road during a suitable break in the traffic. At Atcham, you cross the River Severn using the older (1774) of the two bridges – now closed to motorised traffic.

The route continues in the wide valley of Cound Brook through a sparsely populated agricultural landscape which is only a few miles south of Shrewsbury. You pass near to Condover Hall, which is described in Pevsner's The Buildings of England – Shropshire as 'the grandest Elizabethan House in Shropshire'. It is now a residential activity centre.

A steep climb takes you to Lyth Hill Country Park, from which you get some of the best panoramic views in the county. On a clear day,

The splendid Porthill Bridge over the River Severn

you can see The Wrekin in the east, Wenlock Edge further south and the Stiperstones off to the south-west. After running parallel to the Shropshire Way on a bumpy track, the route rejoins surfaced roads for a mainly downhill return to Shrewsbury. Having crossed the River Severn by pushing your cycle across a footbridge, you can pedal to the finish – back where you started.

Map	Ordnance Survey 1:50,000 Landranger 126
Distance	19.6 miles (31.5km)
Waymarked	No
Gradients	One steep hill
Surface	Mostly asphalt, some gravel, short length of unmetalled track
Shops and refreshments	Shrewsbury
Permits	None required

Access points

There are many alternative places you could start and finish this ride – anywhere alongside the River Severn in Shrewsbury for example. The route as described begins and ends at the Porthill Bridge near The Quarry which is itself close to the centre of Shrewsbury and readily accessible by cycle.

If you drive into Shrewsbury, Frankwell Main near the Theatre Severn is a large and convenient long-stay car park which, at the time of writing, cost £4 for up to 10 hours parking. Exit the car park and proceed past the Theatre Severn to traffic lights. It's then easiest if you dismount and walk across Welsh Bridge before crossing into Victoria Avenue on your right. Cycle along Victoria Avenue to Porthill Bridge.

An alternative start/finish is Shrewsbury Sports Village off Sundorne Road – begin the ride from the 3.38-mile instruction.

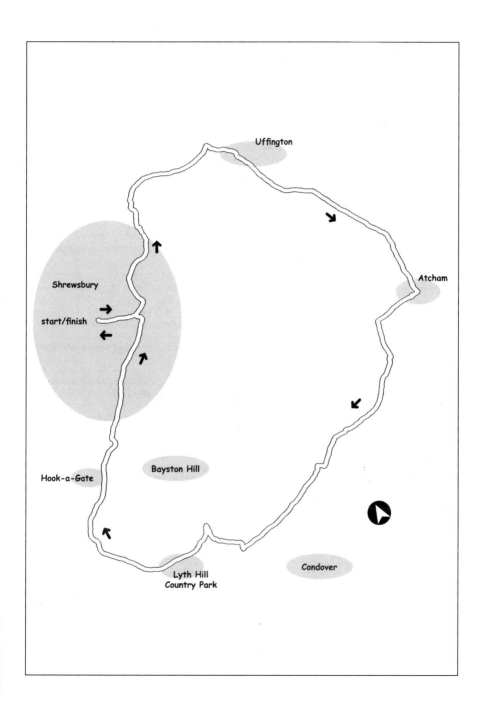

The route

Instruction	Miles	Comments
	0.00	Start beside the River Severn on The Quarry side of the Porthill Bridge – a distinctive suspension bridge for pedestrians. Proceed with the river on your right
Keep right	0.80	Ignore the pathway bearing left – stay alongside the river
	1.50	Ignore turning to left. Continue straight, signposted Sundorne, Harlescott (blue sign)
	1.70	At weir move up onto road and continue beside river
Left	2.10	Follow the road away from the river, signposted Sundorne, Harlescott (blue sign)
Right	2.20	Turn into Darville, signposted Sundorne (blue sign)
Right @ T	2.53	Turn into Millers Green, signposted Sundorne (blue sign)
Right	2.59	At end of cul-de-sac turn into passageway between bungalows, signposted Sundorne (blue sign)
		Follow the cycle path around to the left, signposted National Cycle Route 81 (blue sign)
		Proceed through the underpass then follow the path around to the left
Right @ T	2.72	Turn right at top of slight rise and proceed in to Old Shrewsbury Canal Countryside Heritage Site
Straight	3.00	Ignore left turning, continue straight signposted Uffington (blue sign)
	3.38	Turning on left to Shrewsbury Sports Village – alternative start/finish
Straight	3.80	Exit heritage site near Pimley Manor and continue straight, signposted Wellington etc (blue sign)
	3.93	Proceed under road
Right @ T	4.39	Join road, signposted Wellington, Upton Magna (blue sign)

Instruction	Miles	Comments
		Continue through Uffington
Straight @ x-rds	5.63	Signposted Atcham, Wellington
		Proceed through Berwick Wharf
Straight @ T!	7.66	Care! At the busy B4380 proceed straight across as if going into the hotel car park (you may decide to walk with your cycle), then immediately turn right onto old bridge
Left @ T	7.79	At end of bridge turn left onto minor road then almost immediately...
Right		Not signposted but the road to take is signed as 'Unsuitable for HGVs'
Straight @ x-rds	8.97	Care crossing A-road. Signposted Condover
		Long ascent
Straight @ x-rds	9.55	
Straight @ x-rds	9.80	Give way. Signposted Condover
Right	10.83	Signposted Allfield
Straight @ x-rds	11.62	Give way. Not signposted
Right @ T	11.95	Not signposted
Right @ T	12.46	Give way and care joining A-road. Not signposted. Almost immediately...
Left	12.56	Signposted Little Lyth, Lyth Hill. Signed 'Unsuitable for HGVs'
		Proceed through Little Lyth and continue steep uphill
Left	13.20	At top of hill in the car park take a bridleway to the left signposted Shropshire Way
		Follow a wide, uneven track
Bear right	13.61	At next car park, bear right on to asphalt road and proceed down long descent
Right @ T	15.14	Give way. Signposted National Cycle Route 44 (blue sign)
		Proceed through Hook-a-Gate and into Shrewsbury

Instruction	Miles	Comments
	17.66	At pedestrian crossing just before a roundabout and a Meole Brace park and ride sign, switch to cycle/pedestrian lane on right
Straight @ rbt	17.78	Use the cycle lanes to go straight across a roundabout and then switch to left side of road
		Continue into Shrewsbury, using the cycle lane in due course
Left	18.66	In Coleham high street dismount at a lights-controlled pedestrian crossing. Walk with your cycle along an alleyway between shops towards a footbridge and continue across Greyfriars Bridge
Left	18.75	On the road the other side of the bridge look for a pathway left between bollards, signposted Kingsland, Porthill, Castlefields (blue sign)
		Continue with river on your left
	19.60	Finish at Porthill Bridge

Appendix 1 – useful contacts

National Rail Enquiries **www.nationalrail.co.uk** tel: 08457 484950

Public Transport Information **http://traveline.info** tel: 0871 2002233

Cycling in Shropshire **www.shropshirecycling.co.uk**

Local interest books and maps: Pengwern Books, 9-10 The Market Hall, Shoplatch, Shrewsbury SY1 1QG **www.pengwernbooks.co.uk** tel: 01743 232236

Tourist information, accommodation, places to eat and visit, maps, guides, cycle hire and events:

Shropshire Tourism **www.shropshiretourism.co.uk** tel: 01743 281200
Bridgnorth Visitor Information Centre tel: 01746 763257
Church Stretton Visitor Information Centre tel: 01694 723133
Craven Arms Customer Service Point tel: 01588 676056
Ellesmere Boathouse Visitor Information Centre tel: 01691 622981
Ironbridge Visitor Information Centre tel: 01952 884391
Ludlow Visitor Information Centre tel: 01584 875053
Market Drayton Visitor Information Centre tel: 01630 653114
Much Wenlock Visitor Information Centre tel: 01952 727679
Oswestry Town Visitor Information Centre tel: 01691 662753
Oswestry Visitor Information Centre, Mile End tel: 01691 662488
Shrewsbury Visitor Information Centre tel: 01743 281200
Telford Visitor Information Centre tel: 01952 238008
Whitchurch Visitor Information Centre tel: 01948 664577

To contact any of these Visitor Information Centres by email go to **www.shropshiretourism.co.uk/tourist-information-centre** and follow the links.

Also from Sigma

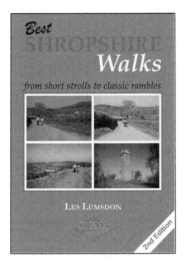

Best Shropshire Walks
2nd Edition
From short strolls to classic rambles
Les Lumsdon

A new revised edition of this much loved guide contains 36 walks, including 12 completely new routes, located in all parts of the county. Several walks feature fine hill walking on the Welsh borders and others start from delightful villages and hamlets in the north and east of the county.
£8.99

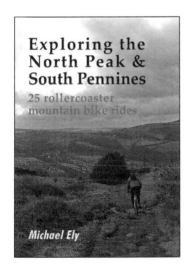

Exploring the North Peak & South Pennines
25 rollercoaster mountain bike rides
Michael Ely

This book will inspire you to pump up the tyres and oil the chain for some excitement, exercise and a feast of rollercoaster riding as you join Michael Ely on some great mountain biking in these Pennine hills. Over 500 miles of riding for the adventurous off-road cyclist that explore the tracks and steep lanes in the Pennine hills. There are twenty-five illustrated rides - with cafe stops half way round - to provide both a challenge and many hours of healthy exercise in classic mountain biking country.
£8.99

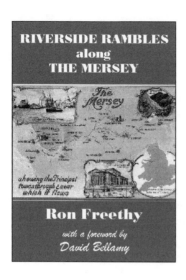

Riverside Rambles along The Mersey
Ron Freethy
with a foreword by David Bellamy

This is far more than a guidebook for walkers, it is also a portrait of one of the world's greatest rivers – once so polluted that Michael Heseltine described the state of the Mersey basin as "an affront to civilised society". Nowadays, however, salmon pass through the estuary, wildlife abounds along the entire catchment area and a rich and diverse coastline attracts a huge variety of birdlife.

Featuring 30 walks short, gentle walks (mostly circular). Explore the unique scenery, ecology and heritage of this area.
£8.99

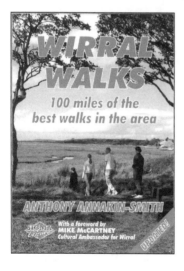

Wirral Walks 2nd Edition
100 miles of the best walks in the area
Anthony Annakin-Smith

A completely revised and updated edition of this popular collection of 25 walks from around 2 to 10 miles, covering a total of 100 miles through the best of the local landscape. The author's careful research highlights the interesting and unusual features seen along each route.
£8.99

Discovering Manchester
2nd Edition
Barry Worthington

This stylish walking guide doubles as a detailed account of the city's architecture, its history and tourism attractions. There are walks throughout Manchester including such major entertainment and cultural centres as the Bridgewater Hall, Urbis, the Museum of Science and Industry, the Lowry and many more. Explore the entire city – from the Corn Exchange to G-Mex, from the Cathedral to Affleck's Palace.

£10.99

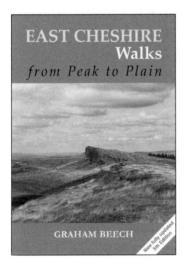

East Cheshire Walks
from Peak to Plain
Graham Beech

East Cheshire is a land of contracts — from rugged hills to gently rolling countryside. Thanks to this variety, there really is something for walkers of all interests and abilities — and *East Cheshire Walks* is by far the most comprehensive guidebook to the area, with almost 40 walks ranging from 3 to 20 miles covering a total of over 250 miles. There are easy ambles in Cheshire's mid-county pasture land, interesting strolls alongside rivers and canals, and a selection of more strenuous hikes in the foothills of the Peak District.

£8.99

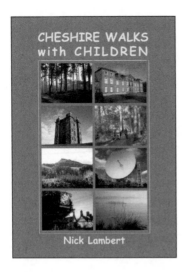

Cheshire Walks With Children 2nd Edition
Nick Lambert

Now completely revised and updated, this was the first in our "walks with children" series and has quickly become a firm favourite. There are 30 walks, ranging in length, together with things to look out for and questions to answer along the way make it an entertaining book for young and old alike.

£8.99

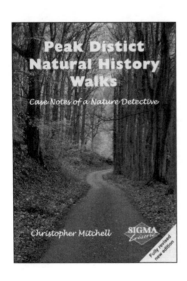

Peak District Walking Natural History Walks
Christopher Mitchell

An updated 2nd Edition with 18 varied walks for all lovers of the great outdoors — and armchair ramblers too! Learn how to be a nature detective, a 'case notes' approach shows you what clues to look for and how to solve them. Detailed maps include animal tracks and signs, landscape features and everything you need for the perfect natural history walk. There are mysteries and puzzles to solve to add more fun for family walks — solutions supplied! Includes follow on material with an extensive Bibliography and 'Taking it Further' sections.

£8.99

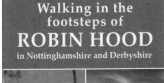

Country Walks in and around Wariwckshire
Ron Weston

This selection of 32 Warwickshire walks takes you on a journey of picturesque villages and historic churches, stately homes and castles, famous gardens and medieval tracks bound together by a superb network of public footpaths and canal towpaths and sometimes spilling over into adjoining counties. All walks in the book are circular, the longest being 5.5 miles and all within a radius of 25 miles from Coventry, with directions of how to get there and where to park.

£8.99

Walking in the footsteps of Robin Hood
in Nottinghamshire and Derbyshire
Jill Armitage

Walking in the Footsteps of Robin Hood roots out the places mentioned in traditional old tales and visits the locations that Robin and his men would have known. Walk through some of middle England's finest countryside on miles of well-marked footpaths to interesting historical sites associated with the outlaw legend. Stoops, caves, wells and stones with the outlaws names have been traced and woven into the walks taking you through Robin Hood country.

£8.99

All-Terrain Pushchair Walks
Cheshire
Norman Buckley

30 graded walks, from level routes around pretty Cheshire villages to more adventurous hikes across the hillsides. Detailed directions and a map are provided for each route, together with some stunning photographs.
£8.99

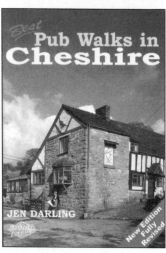

Best Pub Walks in Cheshire
2nd Edition
Jen Darling

This is the second edition of a guidebook to the walks and pubs of Cheshire.
"I was delighted to be asked to put a few words on paper ... this book brings together a series of suggestions for your enjoyment."
– John Ellis, Cheshire Tourism
£8.99